Monie

Hinduism

Monier Williams

Hinduism

ISBN/EAN: 9783337735371

Printed in Europe, USA, Canada, Australia, Japan

Cover: Foto ©Lupo / pixelio.de

NON-CHRISTIAN RELIGIOUS SYSTEMS.

HINDUISM.

BY

MONIER WILLIAMS, M.A., D.C.L.,

HON. DOCTOR IN LAW OF THE UNIVERSITY OF CALCUTTA;

HON. MEMBER OF THE BOMBAY ASIATIC SOCIETY;

BODEN PROFESSOR OF SANSKRIT IN THE UNIVERSITY OF OXFORD.

WITH MAP.

PUBLISHED UNDER THE DIRECTION OF
THE COMMITTEE OF GENERAL LITERATURE AND EDUCATION
APPOINTED BY THE SOCIETY FOR PROMOTING
CHRISTIAN KNOWLEDGE.

SIXTH THOUSAND.

LONDON:
SOCIETY FOR PROMOTING CHRISTIAN KNOWLEDGE.
SOLD AT THE DEPOSITORIES:
77, GREAT QUEEN STREET, LINCOLN'S-INN FIELDS;
4, ROYAL EXCHANGE; 48, PICCADILLY
AND BY ALL BOOKSELLERS.
New York: Pott, Young, & Co.
1878.

CONTENTS.

HINDUISM.

CHAPTER I.

INTRODUCTORY.

THAT part of the great Āryan race which immigrated from Central Asia, through Persia, into India, settled first in the districts near the river Sindhu (now called the Indus).

The Persians pronounced this word Hindhū, and named their Āryan brethren Hindūs. The Greeks, who probably gained their first ideas of India from the Persians, dropped the hard aspirate, and called the Hindūs Ἰνδοί.

After the Hindū Āryans had spread themselves over the plains of the Ganges, the Persians gave the name Hindūstān, or 'abode of the Hindūs,' to the whole district between the Panjāb and Benares, and this name is commonly used, especially by the Musalmāns, for a still more extended region, as far as the Vindhya mountains, and even, less correctly, for other parts of India.

The classical name for India, however, as usually employed in Sanskṛit literature and recognized by the whole Sanskritic races, is *Bhārata* or *Bhārata-varsha* (sometimes *Bhārata-khaṇḍa* or *Kumārikā-khaṇḍa*), 'the country of Bharata,'—a king who appears to have ruled over a large extent of territory in ancient times. Manu's name for the whole central region between the Himālaya and Vindhya mountains is *Āryāvarta*, 'abode of the Āryans,' and this is also a classical appellation for that particular portion of India. Another name for the whole of India, occurring in Sanskṛit poetry, is *Jambu-dvīpa*. Strictly, however, this last is merely a poetical name for the whole earth, of which India was thought to be the most important part.

The population of India amounts to at least 240 millions. So immense an assemblage of beings does not, of course, form one nation. India is almost a continent, like Europe. From the earliest times its richness has attracted successive immigrants and invaders from over-populated and poorer regions, Asiatic and European. Its inhabitants differ as much as the various continental races, and speak languages equally distinct.

First came the primitive immigrants—some Scythian, some Mongolian in their origin—and all falling under the general head of what are called Turanian races, who, migrating from Central Asia and the steppes of Tartary and Tibet, entered India by successive incursions — many of them through the passes adjoining the Panjāb in the North-west, and others through those North-eastern mountain-ravines which mark the course of the river Brahma-putra.

The great Drāviḍian race of the South of India (probably symbolized by the Rāvaṇas and Vibhīshaṇas of epic poetry) represents the most powerful of these early immigrants, and must not be confounded with the more uncivilized aboriginal tribes, inhabiting the hills and the jungles of India, and symbolized in poetry by monkeys.

Next descended on the plains of Hindūstān the first overflowings of the mighty tide of Āryan immigration, caused by the rapid growth and expansion of that primeval family, who called themselves Ārya, or 'noble,' and spoke a language the common source of Sanskṛit, Prākṛit, Zand, Persian, and Armenian in Asia; and of the Hellenic, Italic, Keltic, Teutonic, and Slavonic languages in Europe. Starting at a later period than the primitive Turanian races, but, like them, from some part of the tableland of Central Asia—probably the region surrounding the sources of the Oxus, near Bokhara—they separated into distinct nationalities and peopled Europe, Persia, and India. The Hindū Āryans, after detaching themselves from the Persian branch of the family, settled themselves down as agriculturists (probably at some period between 2000 and 1500 years B.C.) in the districts surrounding the Indus, the five rivers of the Panjāb, and the sacred Sarasvatī—these seven rivers being called *Sapta Sindhu* (in Zand, *Hapta Hendu*). Thence, after a time, they overran by successive irruptions the plains of the Ganges, and spread themselves over the region called Āryāvarta, occupying the whole of Central India, and either coalescing with, and, so to speak, Āryanizing the primitive inhabitants they found there, or driving all who resisted them to the south and to the hills. They were the first promoters of that moral and intellectual progress and civilization in India, of which the Drāviḍian immigrants were the pioneers.

But India, even after its occupation by the great Āryan race, yielded itself up an easy prey to every powerful invader. According to Herodotus, it was subjugated by Darius Hystaspes. This conquest probably occurred about 500 years B.C. It must have been very partial, and did not extend beyond the plains of the Indus, including the Panjāb and Sindh. It was probably followed by considerable subsequent trade and traffic between Persia and India; and to this commercial intercourse may be due the introduction into India of many new ideas—religious and philosophical—and perhaps, also, of the Phœnician alphabet, with which that of some of the Aśoka edicts and inscriptions (about 250 B.C.) is now generally thought to be connected.

The expedition of Alexander the Great to the banks of the Indus, about 327 B.C., is a better authenticated fact. To this invasion is due the first trustworthy information obtained by Europeans concerning the north-westerly portion of India and the region of the five rivers, down which the Grecian troops were conducted in ships by Nearchus. Megasthenes, who was the ambassador of Seleukos Nikator (Alexander's successor, and ruler over the whole region between the Euphrates and Indus, B.C. 312) at the court of Ćandra-gupta (Sandrokottus), in Pāṭaliputra (Patna, or Παλίβοθρα), during a long sojourn in that city collected further information, of which Strabo, Pliny, Arrian, and others availed themselves.

The next immigrants, after a long interval, were the Pārsīs. This small tribe of Persians were driven from their native land by the Muhammadan conquerors under the Ḳhalīf Omar in the seventh century of our era. Adhering to the ancient religion of Persia, which resembled that of the Veda (viz. the worship of one God, symbolized by and manifested in the elements, especially fire), and bringing with them the records of their faith, the Zand-Avastā[1] of their prophet Zoroaster, they settled down in the neighbourhood of Surat about 1100 years ago, and became great merchants and shipbuilders. For two or three centuries we know little of their history. Their religion prevented them from making proselytes, and they never multiplied within themselves to any extent, nor did they amalgamate with the Hindū population, so that even now their number only amounts to about seventy thousand. Nevertheless, from their busy, enterprising habits, in which they emulate Europeans, they form an important section of the population of Bombay and Western India.

Then came the Muhammadans (Arabs, Turks, Afghāns, Moguls, and Persians), who entered India at different times. They now number forty-one millions, or about one-sixth of the entire population; but a large

---

[1] More properly *Avastā-Zand*, text and commentary. The term Zand, which meant commentary, was afterwards applied to the language in which the Pārsī sacred books were written. This Zand language is only separated by a short interval from that of one set of the cuneiform inscriptions, which again was closely followed by Pahlavī.

number of them are descendants of Hindūs converted to Islām. Although they became politically supreme, they were never able to supplant the Hindūs, as these had done their predecessors. Moreover, it was the policy of the Muhammadan conquerors to bend in many points to the prejudices of their Indian subjects. Hence the Muslims of India became to some extent Hindūized, and in language, habits, and character took from the Hindūs more than they imparted.

Nor has the Hindū element lost its ascendency in India, notwithstanding the accession of European ingredients from Portugal, Holland, Denmark, France, and finally England. Albeit the English have spread themselves over the whole country, and achieved a political supremacy greater than that which once belonged to the Musalmāns, yet they have blended far less with the inhabitants. Oil and water do not keep more distinct than do the rulers and the ruled at present in India. The great bulk of the population is still essentially Hindū, and the moral influence of what may be called the Indo-Āryan race is still paramount. Nevertheless, this race by no means forms one united nation. Differences distinguish it, as great as those which once divided and still distinguish European Āryans.

Many causes have combined to produce such diversities. The Indo-Āryans entered India by successive incursions, so that the earlier arrivals differ from the later as widely as Greeks and Romans from Kelts and Teutons. Then, variety of climate has had its effect in modifying character. Moreover, contact with the non-Āryan aboriginal races and with Muhammadans and Europeans has affected the Āryans variously in different parts of India.

As to the non-Āryan races, these also present great differences. They are now generally divided into the two classes of Drāviḍians and Kolarian aborigines, both of which races belong to the division of the world's inhabitants loosely called Turanian; but the first, as already hinted, are by far the most important, from their having attained an independent civilization, and from their having become either wholly or partially Hindūized in religion, manners, and usages, while the Kolarians continue still in their uncivilized aboriginal condition.

Reckoning, therefore, Āryans and non-Āryans, and taking difference of speech as marking and perpetuating separation of populations, though not as necessarily determining distinction of race, we are able to distinguish fourteen separate peoples in India, constituting what might almost be called fourteen separate nationalities. The following are the fourteen different languages which mark them:—

1. *Hindī*, which we may calculate as spoken by about one hundred million persons in Hindūstān proper, including the High Hindī and the Muhammadan form of it (mixed with Persian and Arabic, called Hindūstānī), and various other Hindī dialects, such as Braj, Kanaujī, Mewārī, Old Pūrbī, Awadhī, Bhojpurī, and the Mārwārī of the district of Jodhpur (the most extensive of all the Rājput states), which last dialect is perhaps chiefly deserving of notice.

2. *Bengālī*, spoken by about thirty-six millions in Bengal.

3. *Marāṭhī*, spoken by about fifteen millions in Mahārāshṭra in the Dekhan, including a dialect of it in the Konkan, known as Konkanī.

4. *Gujarātī*, spoken by about seven millions in Gujarāt.

5. *Panjābī*, spoken by about twelve millions in the Panjāb.

6. *Kāśmīrī*, by nearly two millions in Kāśmīr.

7. *Sindhī*, spoken by about two millions in Sindh.

8. *Oriya*, spoken by about five millions in Orissa.

The foregoing eight belong to distinct divisions of the Āryan race, which may be called Indo-Āryan.

Next, taking the non-Āryans, we have six other differences of race, which we may also mark by the names of their languages. In the first place, the four great Drāviḍian races (numbering nearly forty-six million persons), as follows :—

9. *Tamil*, spoken by about fifteen millions, beginning with the northern portion of Ceylon, and extending from Cape Comorin northward along the south of Travancore, and what is called the Karnatic; that is, along the southern part of the Coromandel coast to about a hundred miles north of Madras.

10. *Malayālam*, almost a dialect of Tamil, spoken by nearly four millions in Travancore and along the southern portion of the Malabar coast.

11. *Telugu*, called from its softness the Italian of India, spoken by nearly sixteen millions, from a line north of Madras, along the northern part of the Coromandel coast, or Northern Circars, and over part of the Nizām's territory.

12. *Kanarese*, spoken by rather more than nine

It is a s in Mysore, in the southern portion of the Bombay Presidency, in Kanara, and part of the Malabar coast.

There are two semi-cultivated Drāviḍian dialects, viz. the Tulu, spoken in a small district of Kanara, and the Koorg or Koḍagu, spoken by only 150,000 persons in the hill district to the west of Mysore, which scarcely merit enumeration as languages.

Then comes the chief uncultivated Drāviḍian language, viz.—

13. *Goṇḍ*, spoken by nearly two million aborigines,[1] divided into clans, some of whom are almost savages; while others are comparatively civilized, inhabiting Goṇḍwana in the central provinces. The language of the Goṇḍ race has been lately systematized and expressed in Devanāgarī characters.

The other uncultivated Drāviḍian dialects, viz.—Orāon, Rājmahal, Khoṇḍ, Toḍa and Koṭa, belong to insignificant tribes rather than to races.

Lastly come the wholly uncultivated and barbarous non-Āryan and non-Drāviḍian dialects, called,—

14. *Kolarian*, belonging to the Kols, inhabiting the plateau of Chotā Nāgpur and numbering more than three millions. They speak about seven rude dialects, of which the best known are those of the Kols, the Juāngs (the most primitive tribe in all India), the Santāls, the Mundas, and the Hos.

In the above enumeration are not reckoned the

---

[1] It does not follow that the Goṇḍs are Drāviḍian because their language is so, any more than that the Cornish people are of the English race because they have adopted our language. Dr. Caldwell is my authority for most of these numbers.

languages which belong, so to speak, to t[ions in] fringe of India proper, *e.g.* the Pashtu or Pakhtu of Afghānistān, the Nepālī or Nepālese of Nepāl, the Asamese of Asam, the Burmese of British Burmah, and the Sinhalese of Ceylon; besides more than sixty dialects spoken by tribes inhabiting the mountains of Nepāl, Bhutān, and Asam (some of them coming under what are called the Himalāic family, and many of them more or less connected with Tibetan), making at least one hundred languages and dialects, cultivated and uncultivated, in the whole of India.

But, besides the separation caused by difference of race and language, the divisions and subdivisions of the classes of society within each of the more civilized and cultivated of these several populations crystallized more rapidly in India than in Europe, and with far harder lines of demarcation. Even in districts where the Hindūs are called by one name, and make use of one speech, caste regulations have operated to break them up into an infinite number of independent communities, each priding itself on maintaining its individuality and exclusiveness.

The question then arises how such differences of race, language, and social usages have affected religious creed. It is remarkable that with all their diversities the Hindū populations throughout India have a religious faith which, preserved as it is in one language and one literature, furnishes a good evidence of the original unity of the Indo-Āryan immigrants, while it faithfully reflects the present diversified character of the vast country in which it prevails.

It is a creed based on an original, simple, pantheistic doctrine, but branching out into an endless variety of polytheistic superstitions. Like the sacred fig-tree of India, which from a single stem sends out innumerable branches destined to descend to the ground and become trees themselves, till the parent stock is lost in a dense forest of its own offshoots, so has this pantheistic creed rooted itself firmly in the Hindū mind, and spread its ramifications so luxuriantly that the simplicity of its root-dogma is lost in an exuberant outgrowth of monstrous mythology.

That we may at once briefly formulate this leading dogma, we cannot do better than give its own formula of three words, as stated by its own philosophers, thus,—*Ekam eva advitīyam*, 'There is but one Being, no second'; nothing really exists but the one Universal Spirit called Brahman, and whatever appears to exist independently is identical with that Spirit. This is the uncompromising creed of true Brāhmanism. This, according to the orthodox Hindū philosophy, is the only true Veda. This, at least according to the belief of the generality of educated Hindūs, is the only true knowledge to which the Veda leads.

Popular Hindūism, on the other hand, though supposed to accept this creed as the way of true knowledge (*Jnāna-mārga*) which it admits to be the highest way of salvation, adds to it two other inferior ways:—

1st. Belief in the efficacy of sacrifices, rites, penances, and austerities, which is the *Karma-mārga*, 'way of works.'

2nd. Faith in personal deities, which is the *Bhakti-mārga*, 'way of faith and devotion' (the term *bhakti* corresponding to the Upāsanā of the Upanishads).

Moreover, to account for its polytheism, idol-worship, and system of caste distinctions, popular Hindūism supposes that the one Supreme Being amuses himself by illusory appearances; that he manifests himself variously, as light does in the rainbow; and that all visible and material objects, good and bad, including gods, demons, demi-gods, good and evil spirits, human beings and animals, are emanations from him, and are ultimately to be reabsorbed into his essence.

Hence it may easily be surmised that the road connecting the true knowledge and the popular doctrine must have many windings. And it may with truth be asserted that no description of Hindūism can be exhaustive which does not touch on almost every religious and philosophical idea that the world has ever known.

Starting from the Veda, Hindūism has ended in embracing something from all religions, and in presenting phases suited to all minds. It is all-tolerant, all-compliant, all-comprehensive, all-absorbing. It has its spiritual and its material aspect, its esoteric and exoteric, its subjective and objective, its rational and irrational, its pure and its impure. It may be compared to a huge polygon, or irregular multilateral figure. It has one side for the practical, another for the severely moral, another for the devotional and imaginative, another for the sensuous and sensual, and another for the philosophical and speculative. Those who rest in ceremonial observances find it all-sufficient; those who deny the efficacy of works, and make faith the one requisite, need not wander from its pale; those who are addicted to sensual objects may have their tastes gratified; those who delight in meditating on the nature of God and man, the relation of matter and spirit, the mystery of separate existence, and the origin of evil, may here indulge their love of speculation. And this capacity for almost endless expansion causes almost endless sectarian divisions even among the followers of any particular line of doctrine.

In unison with its variable character and almost universal receptivity, the religious belief of the Hindūs has really no single succinct designation. Looking at it in its pantheistic aspect, we may call it Brāhmanism; in its polytheistic development, Hindūism; but these are not names recognized by the natives.

If, then, such all-comprehensive breadth and diversity are essential features of Hindūism, is it possible to give a concise description of it which shall be intelligible and satisfactory? Only one guide to its intricacies exists.

India, though it has, as we have seen, about one hundred spoken dialects, has only one sacred language and only one sacred literature, accepted and revered by all adherents of Hindūism alike, however diverse in race, dialect, rank, and creed. That language is Sanskṛit, and that literature is Sanskṛit literature—the only repository of the Veda or 'knowledge' in its widest sense; the only vehicle of Hindū theology, philosophy, law, and mythology; the only mirror in which all the creeds opinions, customs, and usages of the Hindūs are faithfully reflected; and (if we may be allowed a fourth metaphor) the only quarry whence the requisite materials may be obtained for improving the vernaculars, or for expressing important religious and scientific ideas.

In Europe literature changes with language. Each modern dialect has its own literature, which is the best representative of the present religious, social, and intellectual condition of the people. To know the Italians, we need not study Latin, when their modern literature is at our command. But the literature of the Hindū vernacular dialects (except, perhaps, that of Tamil) is scarcely yet deserving of the name. In most cases, it consists of mere reproductions of the Sanskṛit. To know the Hindūs, to understand their past and present condition, to reach their very heart and soul, we must study Sanskṛit literature. It is, in truth, even more to India than classical and patristic literature was to Europe at the time of the Reformation. It gives a deeper impress to the Hindū mind, so that every Hindū, however unlettered, is unconsciously affected by it.

There are, however, certain portions of Sanskṛit literature which are, *par excellence*, sacred, and these fall under the two grand heads of *Śruti* and *Smṛiti*.

Śruti—'that which is directly heard or revealed'—includes the three portions of the Veda, viz. Mantra, Brāhmaṇa, and Upanishad, the last being the source of the Darśanas or systems of philosophy.

It is equivalent to direct revelation, and is believed to have no human author.

Smṛiti, 'that which is remembered and handed

down by tradition,' though believed to be founded on this direct revelation, is thought to have been delivered by human authors. In its widest acceptation Smṛiti may be said to denote almost the whole of Post-Vedic literature, under four heads: (A) the six Vedāngas (viz., 1. the *Kalpa*, or *Śrauta-sūtras*, which are rules for applying the Mantra and Brāhmaṇa to Vedic sacrifices; 2. *Śikshā*, or the science of pronunciation; 3. *Chandas*, or metre; 4. *Nirukta*, or exposition of the Veda; 5. *Vyākaraṇa*, or grammar; 6. *Jyotisha*, or astronomy); (B) the Smārta-sūtras, under the two divisions of *Gṛihya-sūtras*, or rules relating to domestic rites; and *Samayāćārika-sūtras*, relating to conventional usages; (C) the Dhārma-śāstras, or 'Law-books,' especially the laws of Manu, Yājnavalkya, and other so-called inspired lawgivers, supposed to have grown out of the Smārta-sūtras; (D) the Bhakti-śāstras, including the *Itihāsas*, or 'legendary poems,' viz., the great epic poem called Mahābhārata, and the other great epic called Rāmāyaṇa (though the latter is rather a *Kāvya* by a known human author, than an Itihāsa, attributed to superhuman authorship); and including also the eighteen *Purāṇas*, or ancient legendary histories, with their train of eighteen Inferior Purāṇas (*Upapurāṇas*), and subsequent *Tantras*.

Although it is not part of our present plan to describe in detail all these divisions of Sanskṛit literature, yet to understand the various phases through which Hindūism has passed, it is essential to have some knowledge of the principal works under four departments—viz., I. The three portions of the Veda,

Mantra, Brāhmaṇa, and Upanishad. II. The Darśanas, or systems of philosophy. III. The Dharma-śāstras. IV. The Bhakti-śāstras. The principal works under these four heads are the best exponents of the different periods of development through which the Hindū religious mind has passed, and which, together, make up Hindūism. The hymns of the Veda are the expression of that early stage of religious progress which may be called physiolatry; the Brāhmaṇas represent ritualism and sacrifice; the Upanishads and Darśanas represent rationalistic and pantheistic philosophy; Manu, Yājnavalkya, and the law-books represent caste and domestic usages; the Itihāsas, Purāṇas, and Tantras represent the principle of faith in and devotion to personal gods. No account of Hindūism can be satisfactory which is not accompanied with translations of occasional passages from some of these representative works.

CHAPTER II.

THE VEDIC HYMNS (*Mantras*).

THE word Veda (meaning 'knowledge') is a term applied to divine *unwritten* knowledge, imagined to have is[illegible] like breath from the self-existent Being ca[illegible], and thought to be itself self-existent. He[illegible] is not unfrequently itself called *Brahm*[illegible] may mean either 'the universally di[illegible] or else 'the spirit of devotion permeatin[illegible]an mind' or 'divine spiritual knowledge.'

This divine knowledge was also connected with *Śabda*, or articulate sound (thought to be eternal), and hence sometimes regarded as an eternal voice (*vāć*) heard by certain holy men called Ṛishis; or, again, as eternal words actually seen by them as well as heard.[1] By them the Divine knowledge—thus supernaturally received through the ear and eye—was transmitted, not in writing, but by constant oral repetition, through a succession of teachers, who claimed to be its rightful recipients, and were thence called *Brāhmans*, that is to say, the repositories both of the divine word, and of the spirit of devotion or prayer.

---

[1] Hence Ṛishi is said to be for Dṛishi, which is from the root *dṛiś*, 'to see.' Of course, this is a mere fanciful theory. The poets themselves frequently hint that the Mantras are their own composition.

Be it noted that we have here a [redacted] inspiration higher even than that advanc[redacted]hammad in explaining the origin of the Ku[redacted] may also note that this idea of an externa[redacted]tural revelation is at the very root of Hindū[redacted]is, indeed, ingrained in the whole Hindū [redacted] The first idea, however, was not that of [redacted]en or *book* revelation. It is very true that reveal[redacted] knowledge was ultimately written down, but even then the reading of it was not encouraged.

Our first step, therefore, in attempting a [redacted] of Hindūism must be to give some noti[redacted] tents of the Veda. To clear the [redacted] separating it into the followi[redacted]stinct subdivisions, all three com[redacted]eral head of *Sruti*, ‘that which [redacted]ed.’

1. *Mantra*, pra[redacted]embodied in texts and metrical [redacted]

2. *Brā*[redacted]stic precept and illustration [redacted]ystical or secret doctrine, appended [redacted]d Brāhmaṇa, and written in prose and oc[redacted] verse.

T[redacted] begin with the Mantra portion. By *Mantra* (literally, ‘the instrument of conveying thought’) is meant any inspired speech or sacred text.

The term is usually applied to those prayers, invocations, and hymns which were addressed to certain deifications of the forces of nature, and ultimately arranged in five Saṃhitās or collections. Though some of the hymns were the property of the Āryan race before they separated, they must have been collected and handed down to us from a period after the Indian branch of the great Indo-European race had finally settled down in the Panjāb and Northern India. Sanskṛit literature, embracing as it does nearly every branch of knowledge, is entirely deficient in one department. It is wholly destitute of trustworthy historical records. Hence, little or nothing is known of the lives of ancient Indian authors, and the date of their most celebrated works cannot be fixed with certainty. A fair conjecture, however, may be arrived at by comparing the most ancient with the more modern compositions, and estimating the period of time required to effect the changes of structure and idiom observable in the language. In this manner we may be justified in assuming that the hymns of the Veda were probably composed by a succession of poets at different dates between 1500 and 1000 years B.C.

Though very unequal in poetical merit, and containing many tedious repetitions and puerilities, they are highly interesting and important, as embodying some of the earliest religious conceptions of the Hindūs, and throwing light on the earliest history and social condition of the Indo-Āryan race.

They are comprised in five principal Saṃhitās, or collections of Mantras, called respectively Ṛić, Yajus (containing two Saṃhitās, Taittirīya and Vājasaneyin), Sāman, and Atharvan. Of these, the Saṃhitā of the Ṛić or Ṛig-veda, containing 1017 hymns, is the oldest and most important. It is a collection of songs in praise of the personified elements. It is not arranged for any ritual purposes, and it includes hymns, many of which may have been sung by our Āryan forefathers before they settled in India.

The Atharva-veda, on the other hand, is generally held to be the most recent, and is, perhaps, the most interesting collection. Though some of its hymns are mere repetitions of those in the Ṛig-veda, it deserves to be called a separate original collection. It had its origin in the growth of a superstitious belief in the power of evil demons, and its verses, including those introduced from the Ṛig-veda, are used in the present day as magical spells and incantations for imprecating or averting evils.

The two so-called Saṃhitās or collections of the Yajur-veda or Sacrificial Veda (viz. the Taittirīya and Vājasaneyin or Black and White Yajus), borrow largely from the Ṛig-veda, and are merely hymns and texts arranged for use at sacrifices, the necessity for which arose after the complicated sacrificial system had been elaborated.

The Sāma-veda again is merely a reproduction of parts of the Ṛig-veda, transposed and arranged for the Soma ceremonies performed by priests called Udgāṭris, as the Yajur-veda was for the sacrifices performed by Adhvaryu priests.[1] The greatest number of its verses are taken from the ninth Maṇḍala of the Ṛig-veda, which is in praise of the Soma plant.

[1] Manu, iv. 123, says: "The Ṛig-veda has the gods for its deities; the Yajur-veda has men for its objects; the Sāma-veda has the Pitṛis or spirits of departed ancestors, therefore its sound is impure." This semblance of impurity is said to be the result of its association with deceased persons, and its repetition at a time of mourning.

To what deities, then, did the Vedic poets address their prayers and hymns?

This is an interesting inquiry, for these were probably the very deities worshipped under similar names by our Āryan progenitors in their primeval home somewhere on the table-land of Central Asia. The answer is, they worshipped those physical forces before which all nations, if guided solely by the light of nature, have in the early period of their life instinctively bowed down, and before which even the more civilized and enlightened have always been compelled to bend in awe and reverence, if not in adoration. Their religion was what may be called in one word *physiolatry*.

To our Āryan forefathers in their Asiatic home God's power was exhibited in the forces of nature even more strikingly than to ourselves. Lands, houses, flocks, herds, men, and animals were more frequently than in Western climates at the mercy of winds, fire, and water, and the sun's rays possessed a potency quite beyond the experience of any European country. We cannot be surprised, then, that these forces were regarded as actual manifestations either of one deity in different moods or of separate rival deities contending for supremacy. Nor is it wonderful that these mighty agencies should have been at first poetically personified, and afterwards, when invested with forms, attributes, and individuality, worshipped as distinct gods. It was only natural, too, that a varying supremacy and varying honours should have been accorded to each deified force—to the air, the rain, the storm, the sun, or fire—according to the special atmospheric influences to which particular localities were exposed, or according to the seasons of the year when the dominance of each was to be prayed for or deprecated.

This was the religion represented in the Vedas, and was probably the primitive creed of the Indo-Āryans about twelve or thirteen centuries before Christ. The first forces deified seem to have been those manifested in the sky and air. These were at first generalized under one simple but rather vague personification, as was natural in the earliest attempts at giving shape to religious ideas. In the Veda this unity soon diverged into various ramifications. Only a few of the hymns appear to contain the simple conception of one divine self-existent Being, and even in these the idea of one God present in all nature is somewhat nebulous and undefined. Perhaps the most ancient and beautiful deification was that of Dyaus, 'the sky,' as Dyaush-pitar, 'Heavenly Father' (the Zeus or Ju-piter of the Greeks and Romans). Then, closely connected with Dyaus, was a goddess Aditi, 'the Infinite Expanse,' conceived of subsequently as the mother of all the gods. Next came a development of the same conception called Varuṇa, 'the Investing Sky,' said to answer to Ahura Mazda, the Ormazd of the ancient Persian (Zand) mythology, and to the Greek Οὐρανός, but a more spiritual conception, leading to a worship which rose to the nature of a belief in the great Πατὴρ ἡμῶν ὁ ἐν τοῖς οὐρανοῖς. This Varuṇa, again, was soon thought of in connection with another vague personification called Mitra (= the Persian *Mithra*), 'god of day.' After a time these impersonations of the celestial sphere were felt to be too vague to suit the growth of religious ideas in ordinary minds. Soon, therefore, the great investing firmament was resolved into separate cosmical entities with separate powers and attributes. First, the watery atmosphere, personified under the name of Indra, ever seeking to dispense his dewy treasures, though ever restrained by an opposing force or spirit of evil called Vṛitra; and, secondly, the wind, thought of either as a single personality named Vāyu, or as a whole assemblage of moving powers coming from every quarter of the compass, and impersonated as Maruts, or 'Storm-gods.' At the same time the once purely celestial Varuṇa became relegated to a position among seven secondary deities of the heavenly sphere called Ādityas (afterwards increased to twelve, and regarded as diversified forms of the sun in the several months of the year), and subsequently to a dominion over the waters when they had left the air and rested on the earth.

Of these separately deified physical forces by far the most favourite object of adoration was the deity supposed to yield the dew and rain. Indra is the Jupiter Pluvius of early Indian mythology, and he is the principal divinity of Vedic worshippers, if, at least, the mere number of prayers and hymns addressed to him is to be taken as an indication of his superiority.

What, however, could rain effect without the aid of heat?—a force the intensity of which must have impressed an Indian mind with awe. Hence, the second great god of Vedic worshippers and the most important in connection with sacrificial rites, is Agni (Latin, *Ignis*), 'the god of fire.' Even Sūrya, 'the sun' (Greek, ἥλιος), who is generally the first and most important god in all Pagan systems as the supposed source of heat, generation, and growth, was sometimes regarded by the Hindūs as another form of fire, a manifestation of the same divine energy in the heavens.

These three, Indra, Agni, and Sūrya constitute the Vedic chief triad of gods.

Another deity, Ushas, 'goddess of the dawn,' the ἠώς of the Greeks, was naturally connected with the sun, and regarded as daughter of the sky. Two other deities, the Aśvins, were fabled as twin sons of the Sun (by his wife Aśvinī), ever young and handsome, travelling in a golden car, and precursors of Ushas the dawn. They are sometimes called Dasras, as divine physicians, 'destroyers of diseases'; sometimes Nāsatyas, as 'never untrue.' They appear to have been personifications of two luminous points or rays, imagined to precede the break of day.

And here, it should be stated, that the earth, under the name of Pṛithivī, 'the broad one,' receives a certain share of honour as one of the primitive goddesses of the Veda, being thought of as the mother of all beings. Moreover, various deities were regarded as the progeny resulting from the fancied union of earth with Dyaus, 'heaven,' just as much of the later mythology may be explained by a supposed blending of the male and female principles in nature. But it is remarkable that as religious worship became of a more selfish character, the earth, being more evidently under man's control, and not seeming to need propitiation so urgently as the more uncertain air, fire, and water, lost importance, and was rarely adored in prayer or hymn.

If to the foregoing enumeration of the gods of the Veda be added the name of Yama, the god of departed spirits, and the appointed judge and punisher of the dead, the principal deities to whom the Mantras of the Vedic hymns were addressed, will then have been stated.

It should be observed that the native commentaries on the Veda often allude to thirty-three gods, which number is also mentioned in the Ṛig-veda (I. 34, 11; I. 45, 2). This is a multiple of three, which is a sacred number constantly appearing in the Hindū religious system.[1] It is probable, indeed, that although the Tri-mūrti is not named in the Vedic hymns, yet the Veda is the real source of this Triad of personifications, afterwards so conspicuous in Hindū mythology. This much, at least, is clear, that the Vedic poets exhibited a tendency to group all the forces and energies of nature under three heads, and the assertion that the number of the gods was thirty-three, amounted to saying that each of the three leading personifications was capable of eleven modifications. There can be no doubt that a change of name in Hindū mythology does not necessarily imply the creation of a new deity. Indra, Vāyu, the Maruts and Rudras, appear to have been all forms

---

[1] For example, there are three Vedas, three Mārgas or ways of salvation, three Guṇas or fetters of the soul, three principal castes, three eyes in Śiva's forehead, three objects of human pursuit, three worlds, &c.

and modifications of each other, and these with different names in the later mythology were gathered into the one personification Śiva. Similarly, Sūrya, the sun, had various forms, such as Ādityas; and one of these, named Vishṇu, in the Ṛig-veda, led to the second member of the Tri-mūrti, while Agni, fire or heat, the great generator of life, who is called in the Ṛig-veda 'father of the sacrifice,' and is himself said to have a triple essence, and was apparently often identified by his worshippers with the Supreme Being, easily passed into the first member of the Tri-mūrti, Brahmā, or when the worship of Brahmā seemed to give place to that of Śiva, into one aspect of this latter deity.

The following are free translations (taken from 'Indian Wisdom') of portions of the most remarkable hymns in the Ṛig-veda. The first (Maṇḍala, x. 129) attempts to describe the mystery of creation thus:—

In the beginning there was neither nought nor aught;
Then there was neither sky nor atmosphere above.
What then enshrouded all this teeming universe?
In the receptacle of what was it contained?
Was it enveloped in the gulf profound of water?
Then was there neither death nor immortality;
Then there was neither day, nor night, nor light, nor darkness,
Only the Existent One breathed calmly, self-contained.
Nought else but he there was—nought else above, beyond.
Then first came darkness hid in darkness, gloom in gloom;
Next all was water, all a chaos indiscrete,
In which the One lay void, shrouded in nothingness.
Then turning inwards, he by self-developed force
Of inner fervour and intense abstraction, grew.
First in his mind was formed Desire, the primal germ
Productive, which the Wise, profoundly searching, say
Is the first subtle bond, connecting Entity
With Nullity.

In this hymn we perceive the first dim outline of the remarkable idea that the Creator willed to produce the universe through the agency and co-operation of a female principle—an idea which afterwards acquired more definite shape in the supposed marriage of heaven and earth before alluded to. The same idea assumed a character of its own in the Sānkhya philosophy (as we shall see hereafter), and gathered such strength subsequently that every principal deity in the later mythology has his feminine counterpart, who shares the worship paid to the male god, and who sometimes receives the greater homage of the two. That this idea is not fully developed in the Ṛig-veda is proved by the fact that with the exception of Aditi, Ushas, and Pṛithivī, most of the goddesses are insignificant. The wives of the chief gods, such as Indrāṇī, Agnāyī, Aśvinī, Varuṇānī, &c., are not associated with their husbands as objects of worship, and even Lakshmī and Sarasvatī, though named, are not adored.[1]

The next specimen is from the 121st hymn of the 1st Maṇḍala. Like the preceding, it furnishes a good argument for those who maintain that the original faith of the Hindūs was monotheistic:—

What god shall we adore with sacrifice?
Him let us praise, the golden child that rose
In the beginning, who was born the lord—

[1] In the Sāma-veda (viii. p. 420) the idea is more fully expressed: "He felt not delight, being alone. He wished another, and instantly became such. He caused his own self to fall in twain, and thus became husband and wife. He approached her, and thus were human beings produced."

The one sole lord of all that is—who made
The earth, and formed the sky, who giveth life,
Who giveth strength, whose bidding gods revere,
Whose hiding-place is immortality,
Whose shadow, death; who by his might is king
Of all the breathing, sleeping, waking world.
Where'er let loose in space, the mighty waters
Have gone, depositing a fruitful seed,
And generating fire, there *he* arose
Who is the breath and life of all the gods,
Whose mighty glance looks round the vast expanse
Of watery vapour—source of energy,
Cause of the sacrifice—the only God
Above the gods.

Here follow portions of other hymns to Varuṇa, and to the Vedic triad, Indra, Agni, and Sūrya :—

The mighty Varuṇa, who rules above, looks down
Upon these worlds, his kingdom, as if close at hand.
When men imagine they do ought by stealth, he knows it.
No one can stand, or walk, or softly glide along,
Or hide in dark recess, or lurk in secret cell,
But Varuṇa detects him, and his movements spies.
Two persons may devise some plot, together sitting,
And think themselves alone; but he, the king is there—
A third—and sees it all. His messengers descend
Countless from his abode, for ever traversing
This world, and scanning with a thousand eyes its inmates.
Whate'er exists within this earth, and all within the sky,
Yea, all that is beyond, king Varuṇa perceives.
The winkings of men's eyes are numbered all by him :
He wields the universe as gamesters handle dice.

Indra, twin-brother of the god of fire,
When thou wast born, thy mother Aditi,
Gave thee, her lusty child, the thrilling draught
Of mountain-growing Soma—source of life
And never-dying vigour to thy frame.

Thou art our guardian, advocate, and friend,
A brother, father, mother—all combined.
Most fatherly of fathers, we are thine,
And thou art ours. Oh ! let thy pitying soul
Turn to us in compassion when we praise thee,
And slay us not for one sin or for many.
Deliver us to-day, to-morrow, every day.
Vainly the demon[1] dares thy might; in vain
Strives to deprive us of thy watery treasures.
Earth quakes beneath the crashing of thy bolts.
Pierced, shattered lies the foe—his cities crushed,
His armies overthrown, his fortresses
Shivered to fragments; then the pent-up waters,
Released from long imprisonment, descend
In torrents to the earth, and swollen rivers,
Foaming and rolling to their ocean-home,
Proclaim the triumph of the Thunderer.

Agni, thou art a sage, a priest, a king,
Protector, father of the sacrifice.
Commissioned by us men, thou dost ascend
A messenger, conveying to the sky
Our hymns and offerings. Though thy origin
Be threefold, now from air, and now from water,
Now from the mystic double Araṇi,
Thou art thyself a mighty god, a lord,
Giver of life and immortality,
One in thy essence, but to mortals three;
Displaying thine eternal triple form,
As fire on earth, as lightning in the air,
As sun in heaven. Thou art the cherished guest
In every household—father, brother, son,
Friend, benefactor, guardian, all in one.
Deliver, mighty lord, thy worshippers,
Purge us from taint of sin, and when we die,
Deal mercifully with us on the pyre,

---

[1] The demon Vṛitra. See p. 23.

Burning our bodies with their load of guilt,
But bearing our eternal part on high
To luminous abodes and realms of bliss,
For ever there to dwell with righteous men.

Behold the rays of Dawn, like heralds, lead on high
The Sun, that men may see the great all-knowing god.
The stars slink off like thieves, in company with Night,
Before the all-seeing eye, whose beams reveal his presence,
Gleaming like brilliant flames, to nation after nation.
Sūrya, with flaming locks, clear-sighted god of day,
Thy seven ruddy mares bear on thy rushing car.
With these thy self-yoked steeds, seven daughters of thy chariot,
Onward thou dost advance. To thy refulgent orb,
Beyond this lower gloom, and upward to the light
Would we ascend, O Sun, thou god among the gods.

We may add a few verses from the celebrated Purusha-sūkta, one of the most recent hymns of the Ṛig-veda (Maṇḍala, x. 90). It will serve to illustrate the gradual sliding of Hindū monotheism into pantheism, and the first foreshadowing of the idea of sacrifice, as well as the institution of caste,[1] which for so many centuries has held India in bondage :—

The embodied spirit has a thousand heads,
A thousand eyes, a thousand feet, around
On every side enveloping the earth,
Yet filling space no larger than a span.
He is himself this very universe;
He is whatever is, has been, and shall be;
He is the lord of immortality.
All creatures are one-fourth of him, three-fourths

[1] This hymn (generally admitted to be a comparatively modern production) is the only hymn in the Ṛig-veda which alludes to the distinctions of caste.

Are that which is immortal in the sky.
From him, called Purusha, was born Virāj,
And from Virāj was Purusha produced,
Whom gods and holy men made their oblation.
With Purusha as victim, they performed
A sacrifice. When they divided him,
How did they cut him up? What was his mouth?
What were his arms? and what his thighs and feet?
The Brāhman was his mouth, the kingly soldier
Was made his arms, the husbandman his thighs,
The servile Śūdra issued from his feet.

Be it observed, in conclusion, that the above examples would, if taken alone, encourage a very false estimate of the merits of the Vedic Mantras. Although the majority of the Hindūs believe that the several Saṃhitās of the Veda, and especially that of the Ṛig-veda, contain all that is good, great, and divine, yet these collections of hymns will be found, when taken as a whole, to abound more in puerile ideas than in striking thoughts and lofty conceptions. Nor will they be found to support any of those objectionable practices, superstitions, and opinions of the present day for which they were once, through ignorance of their contents, supposed to be an authority. The Vedic hymns contain no allusion to the doctrine of transmigration of souls, which is a conspicuous characteristic of the Hindū creed in the later system. Nor do they afford any sanction to the prohibition of widow-marriages, the encouragement of child-marriages, the iron rules of caste, and the interdiction of foreign travel. Nor is there in them any evidence that the personifications of the forces of nature were represented by images or symbols carved out of wood or stone. On the contrary, it may be taken as almost certain that there were no idols and no temples to hold images in Vedic times.

That the social condition of the people was by no means low, and that they had attained to some degree of civilization, may be inferred from various allusions in the hymns. It is evident that the chief riches of the newly-arrived Indo-Āryans consisted in flocks and herds; that they understood the principles of agriculture; that they were able to build towns and fortified places; that they had some knowledge of various arts and sciences and of working in metals; that they engaged in philosophical speculations; that they had rulers; that they were separated into classes, though they were not yet divided off by hard lines of caste; that polygamy existed, though monogamy was the rule; that they killed animals for sacrifices; that they were in the habit of eating animal food, and did not even object to the flesh of cows; that they were fond of gambling, and indulged in intoxicating beverages.

We may also gather that just as the children of Israel found the land of Canaan pre-occupied by Hittites, Perizzites, and Philistines, so the immigrating Āryans, when they advanced into India, found the soil held by Scythian and aboriginal races, variously called Dasyus, Anāryas, Nishādas, and Drāviḍas, who, from long exposure to the Indian sun, and perhaps from intermarriage with even more primitive and (as some believe) *Negroid* aboriginal tribes, had become almost as dark-complexioned as Africans.

CHAPTER III.

THE BRĀHMAṆAS AND THE SACRIFICIAL SYSTEM.

Having thus endeavoured to explain the nature of the Vedic hymns, we now turn to the second division of the Veda called Brāhmaṇa, which, in relation to the rise of Brāhmanical authority, the elaboration of the idea of sacrifice, and the development of the ritual, is more important than the Mantra portion.

What, then, are the Brāhmaṇas?

They are intended, as their name implies, for the Brāhmans, and especially for their use in conducting the complicated sacrificial ceremonies. Just as the Mantras are the representatives of the nature-worship of the Ṛishis which was developed in the Panjāb, so the Brāhmaṇas are the exponents of the ritualism of the Brāhmans, developed when they had settled in North-western Hindūstān.

Their chief aim is to serve as guides or directories for the employment of the Mantras at sacrifices. But they do more than this. They speculate as to the meaning and effect of using particular verses and metres, and give explanations of the origin, import, and conduct of the sacrifices, frequently intermixing illustrations in the shape of legends and old stories. The rambling discursiveness of these compositions (the oldest of which may have been written in the seventh century B.C.) made them practically useless as directories to the ritual until they themselves were furnished with guides in the form of Sūtras or aphoristic rules.[1]

Each of the Saṃhitās, or collections of Mantras, has its own Brāhmaṇas. Thus the Ṛig-veda has the Aitareya-brāhmaṇa (perhaps the oldest) and the Kaushītaki (or Śānkhyāyana)-brāhmaṇa. The two collections of the Yajur-veda have the Taittirīya-brāhmaṇa and the Śatapatha-brāhmaṇa, which last, belonging to the Vājasaneyi-saṃhitā, is perhaps one of the most complete of these productions. The Sāma-veda has eight Brāhmaṇas, of which the two best known are the Prauḍha (= Panća-vinśa, Tāṇḍya) and the Shadvinśa. The Atharva-veda has the Gopatha-brāhmaṇa.

Though much of the matter of these treatises is little better than the silliest sacerdotalism, yet they furnish valuable materials to any one interested in tracing the rise and progress of Brāhmanism, and the development of its sacrificial system.

We may observe that the division of the people into the four great classes of *Brāhmaṇas*, priests;

---

[1] These were called Kalpa or Srauta-sūtras. Others, which were guides to domestic ceremonies, were called Smārta or Gṛihya-sūtras (see p. 15). The word Sūtra is derived from the root *siv*, 'to sew,' and means 'a string of rules.' A Sūtra should properly be expressed with the utmost possible brevity. It is frequently nothing but a few suggestive memorial words used like algebraic signs, and unintelligible without a key. In later times, Sūtra works are merely collections of formulated precepts, adapted to serve as manuals to particular systems of teaching, whether in ritual, philosophy, law, or grammar.

Kshatriyas, soldiers; *Vaiśyas*, agriculturists; and *Śūdras*, servants,—as foreshadowed in the Purusha-sūkta of the Ṛig-veda (see p. 30),—was at this period more thoroughly established, though the rules of caste as laid down in the laws of Manu (see p. 57) were not yet generally in force. It may be noted, too, that the Brāhmaṇas express belief in a future state more positively than the Mantras. They assert that a recompense awaits all beings in the next world according to their conduct in this. But the doctrine of transmigration, which became afterwards an essential element of Hindūism, is not yet fully developed, though hinted at in the Śatapatha-brāhmaṇa (xi. 6. 1. 1).[1]

One of the most remarkable ideas to be found in the Brāhmaṇas is that the gods were merely mortals till they extorted immortality from the Supreme Being by sacrifices and austerities. This is expressed in the following free translation of a passage of the Śatapatha-brāhmaṇa:—

> The gods lived constantly in dread of Death—
> The mighty Ender—so with toilsome rites
> They worshipped and repeated sacrifices
> Till they became immortal. Then the Ender
> Said to the gods, 'As ye have made yourselves
> Imperishable; so will men endeavour
> To free themselves from me; what portion then
> Shall I possess in man?' The gods replied,
> 'Henceforth no being shall become immortal
> In his own body; this his mortal frame

[1] Animals and plants are described as revenging, in a future state of existence, injuries inflicted on them by men in this life.

> Shalt thou still seize ; this shall remain thy own.
> He who through knowledge or religious acts
> Henceforth attains to immortality
> Shall first present his body, Death, to thee.'

And again in the Taittirīya-brāhmaṇa,—'By means of the sacrifice the gods obtained heaven.'

But a still more remarkable conception is that first found in the Purusha-sūkta of the Ṛig-veda, already quoted, which represents the gods as sacrificing *Purusha*, the primeval Male, supposed to be coeval with the Creator.

This idea is even more remarkably developed in the Tāṇḍya-brāhmaṇas thus :—

'The lord of creatures (*prajā-pati*) offered himself a sacrifice for the gods.'

And again, in the Śatapatha-brāhmaṇa, 'He who, knowing this, sacrifices with the *Purusha-medha*, or sacrifice of the primeval male, becomes everything.'

Surely, in these mystical allusions to the sacrifice of a representative man, we may perceive traces of the original institution of sacrifice as a divinely-appointed ordinance typical of the one great voluntary sacrifice of the Son of God for the sins of the world.[1]

Whether they point to the actual sacrifice of human beings as part of the early Indo-Āryan system, admits of question. Doubtless the practice of human sacrifice was eventualiy introduced ; and both children

---

[1] Professor Banerjea (p. 204 of his 'Arian Witness') thinks that it would not be easy to account for the genesis of such an idea, except on the assumption of some primitive tradition of the 'Lamb slain from the foundation of the world.'

and adults were immolated as victims at the altars of the bloody goddess Kālī in her numerous local forms. Such sacrifices were once regarded as the only means of propitiating her on occasions of great public calamities, when she was supposed to send blight, disease, and pestilence; and for a long period they continued to be secretly, if not openly, perpetrated in certain districts of India. They were, at any rate, extensively prevalent among the wild and uncultivated Drāviḍian and aboriginal tribes; many of whose practices were adopted by the Hindūs, and contributed largely to mould the Vedic religion into its subsequent form.

That human sacrifice was not at least unknown at the time the Aitareya-brāhmaṇa was composed is indicated by the story of Śunaḥśepha, of which the following is the briefest possible epitome:—

King Hariśćandra had no son; he then prayed to Varuṇa, promising, that if a son were born to him, he would sacrifice the child to the god. Then a son was born to him called Rohita. When Rohita was grown up, his father one day told him of the vow he had made to Varuṇa and bade him prepare to be sacrificed. The son objected to be killed, and ran away from his father's house. For six years he wandered in the forest and at last met a starving Brāhman. Him he persuaded to sell one of his sons named Śunaḥśepha, for a hundred cows. This boy was bought by Rohita and taken to Hariśćandra and about to be sacrificed to Varuṇa as a substitute for Rohita, when, on praying to the gods with verses from the Veda, he was released by them.

Nevertheless, it is clear from the following passage in the same Brāhmaṇa that the sacrifice of human beings was really so repugnant to Āryan instincts that it did not long retain the direct sanction of the Brāhmans :—

The gods killed a man for their victim. But from him thus killed, the part which was fit for a sacrifice went out and entered a horse. Thence, the horse became an animal fit for being sacrificed. The gods then killed the horse, but the part of it for being sacrificed went out of it and entered an ox. The gods then killed the ox, but the part of it fit for being sacrificed went out of it and entered a sheep. Thence it entered a goat. The sacrificial part remained for the longest time in the goat; thence, it became pre-eminently fit for being sacrificed!

This passage indicates that whatever the actual practice may have been—the desire of the Brāhmans was to abolish human sacrifice, and substitute in its place the sacrifice of animals, four kinds of which are enumerated—horses, oxen, sheep, and goats,—in the regular order of their fitness for immolation—according to some inherent efficacy in each class.[1] It is remarkable that in Vedic times, even a cow (called *anustaraṇī*), was sometimes killed,[2] and goats, as is well known, are still sacrificed to the goddess Kālī.

In the Ṛig-veda, the *Aśva-medha* or 'horse-sacrifice,' is made an important ceremony, and hymns 162 and 163 in Maṇḍala I. were used at this rite, which was regarded as the chief of all animal sacrifices.

Indeed, it is essential to a clear comprehension of Brāhmanism and Hindūism, that the exact nature and

---

[1] In the Vājasaneyi-Saṃhitā of the White Yajur-veda two hundred and ten different kinds of victims for sacrifice are enumerated. In Manu, v. 42, it is stated that animals duly sacrificed are conveyed to heavenly mansions.

[2] The killing of a cow and burning it with the body of a deceased person is described by Āśvalāyana.

meaning of sacrifice, as employed by the Hindūs, should be impressed on the mind at the very outset. The idea of the need of sacrificial acts of some kind, is ingrained in their whole system. It is one of the earliest that appears in Indian religious works, and no literature —not even the Jewish—contains so many words relating to sacrifice as Sanskṛit. But the oldest form of Vedic sacrifice was not piacular. It consisted in the mere dedication of offerings of food to the gods. This was generally done by oblations of butter, &c., in fire, or by pouring out libations of the juice of the Soma plant, which were supposed to nourish and exhilarate the deities, especially Indra.[1] In fact, one object of a Hindū's sacrifices and oblations, whether in Vedic or post-Vedic times, has always been, and still continues to be, the supposed actual nourishment of the gods, by the aroma or essence of the substances offered;[2] food being regarded as a necessity of their being.[3] Thus, in the Vishṇu-purāṇa we read, 'By sacrifices the gods are nourished.'

---

[1] There are two Sanskṛit roots for 'to sacrifice': *hu* (=an older *dhu*=θυ) and *yaj*. The first is restricted to oblations of clarified butter in fire; the latter, which means 'to worship,' is applied to sacrificing generally. Besides these two roots, the root *su* is used for offering libations with the juice of the Soma.

[2] The spirits of departed ancestors are also supposed to be refreshed and nourished by libations of water, and offerings of food (Manu, iii. 237).

[3] Sleep seems also necessary to them. From a particular day in the month Āshāḍha to a particular day in Kārttika the gods are supposed to sleep. Vishṇu wakes up on the eleventh day of the light half of Kārttika. Indra is said to rise on the new moon of Āśvina, celebrated as *Śakrotthāna;* and before Durgā is worshipped at the autumnal Durgā-pūjā she must be

But the idea of expiation was gradually introduced even in Vedic times. The sacrificer was mystically identified with the victim, which was regarded as the ransom for sin, and the instrument of its annulment. In the Tāṇḍya-brāhmaṇa, we read,—

O thou limb of the victim now consigned to the fire, thou art the expiation for sins committed by the gods, by the fathers (our deceased ancestors), by men, by ourselves. Whatever sin we have committed, sleeping or waking, knowing or unknowing, thou art the expiation for that.

And here we have to note a third object of sacrifice. Besides the wish to nourish the gods with the savour of the material substances offered, and besides the desire for expiation, resulting from substituted suffering, the sacrificer might have a third aim. It was believed possible by sacrifice to acquire super-human power, and to wrest from the gods any desired boon, or object of ambition, however difficult of attainment. This could also be effected through the practice of austerities, but wealthy individuals who had large resources in money and priests at command, relied more on the efficacy of particular sacrifices (such as the Jyotishṭoma, Agnishṭoma, Vājapeya, &c.), elaborately conducted by Brāhmans with the punctilious observance of a complicated ritual, and the distribution of largesses to the officiating priests. According to the popular creed, a hundred horse-sacrifices so conducted, exalted the sacrificer to the rank of a powerful deity, and even entitled him to displace Indra himself from

---

awaked, and a ceremony called *Bodhana*, 'arousing of the goddess,' takes place. On the other hand, one of the characteristics of the gods is said to be that they never wink.

the dominion of heaven. Hence, the very gods for whose nourishment and propitiation sacrifices were intended, were thought to be jealous of over-zeal displayed by pious individuals in multiplying sacrificial rites, and were even said to put impediments in their way. Nevertheless, in spite of such supposed opposition to excessive piety, the number of sacrificers and sacrifices of all kinds, increased in India.

In fact, for the whole Brāhmaṇa period of Hindūism (probably from 800 to 500 B.C.), the need of propitiatory offerings through the oblation of food in fire and immolation of animals remained a central doctrine of Brāhmanism. Thousands of animals were killed every day. The land was saturated with blood The greater the number of the sacrifices and the more elaborate the ritual, the greater the need for a more complete organization of priests. In this manner the whole Brāhmanical sacrificial system, of which the Brāhmaṇa portion of the Veda is the expression and exponent, was overdone. People became wearied and disgusted with sacrifices, sacrificers, and sacrificing priests.

Then, about five centuries before our era, the reformer Buddha appeared, and about contemporaneously with him various Brāhman sages, stimulated by his example and perhaps by that of others who preceded him,[1] thought out what are called the orthodox systems of Hindū philosophy. The bolder reformers found ready listeners when they began to

[1] There is no reason for supposing that the Buddha was the first freethinker and philosopher that India produced. He himself taught that other Buddhas had preceded him.

preach the impossibility of vicarious suffering; the transmigration of souls; the necessity that every man should suffer himself, and in his own person, for his own sins, either in this or future lives; the unity of all being; the identity of the human soul with the Divine, and the consequent absurdity of caste-distinctions. All idea of the need of propitiatory sacrifice was by them rejected; for when every man was believed to be a part of God, what necessity was there that God should propitiate Himself? If a portion of the One Universal Soul chose for a time to ignore itself, to enclose itself in a body, to fetter itself with actions and their inevitable results, the consequent suffering could only be borne by itself in its passage through numerous existences, and there could be no release—no final emancipation—till action ceased, and the consciousness of identity with the one universal soul returned. Hence the gradual diminution of animal sacrifices throughout India, except at the altars of the fierce goddess Kālī or Durgā, who is supposed to delight in blood, and, if satiated by the immolation of goats and buffaloes, to abstain from causing further destruction. But at no other temples are victims now killed, and even such propitiatory slaughtering of animals is utterly repugnant to the present feelings and opinions of the educated Hindūs. Such was the great revolution effected by Buddha and the Brāhman philosophers together.

It will be necessary to give fuller consideration to the new ideas thus introduced into Brāhmanism. But before describing them more in detail, we must first glance at the third or Upanishad portion of the Veda, which was really the source whence they sprang.

CHAPTER IV.

THE UPANISHADS AND BRĀHMANICAL PHILOSOPHY.

THE third division of the Veda is called *Upanishad*, which implies something that underlies the surface. The doctrine contained in these treatises does in fact lie under the whole Hindū system. Not only are the Upanishads as much *Śruti*, or 'revelation' as the Mantra and Brāhmaṇa portion of the Veda, but they are practically the only part of the Veda much studied and appealed to by educated Hindūs in the present day.

To understand this, we must bear in mind that Indian authorities separate the Veda into two divisions. The first is called *Karma-kāṇḍa*, 'the department of works.' This embraces both Mantra and Brāhmaṇa, and is for that vast majority of persons who are unable to conceive of religion, except as a process of laying up merit by prayers, sacrifices, rites, and austerities. For these the one God assumes various forms, to any of which worship may be addressed and honour paid.

The second is called *Jnāna-kāṇḍa*—'the department of knowledge.' This is taught in the Upanishads and is for that select few who are capable of understanding the true doctrine.

We have already seen (p. 11) that the creed of the man who is said to possess the true knowledge is singularly simple. He believes that there is but one real Being in the universe, which Being also constitutes the universe.

This pantheistic doctrine is everywhere traceable in some of the more ancient Upanishads, though often wrapped up in mysticism and allegory. A list of about 150 of these treatises is given, most of which are written in prose with occasional variations in verse. The absence of historical records in India makes it impossible to fix the date of any of them with more certainty than that of the Mantras. Their style is, however, less archaic, and not very different from that of classical Sanskṛit. Some of the more ancient are probably as old as the sixth century B.C. These are appended to the Āraṇyakas—certain chapters of the Brāhmaṇas, so awe-inspiring and profound, that they were required to be read in the solitude of forests. Properly each Brāhmaṇa had its Āraṇyakas; but the philosophical ideas they contained were so mixed up with extraneous subjects, that the chapters called Upanishads were added with the object of investigating more definitely such abstruse problems as the origin of the universe, the nature of the deity, the nature of the human soul, and the reciprocal connexion of spirit and matter.

The names of the ten most important Upanishads are the *Īśa* (actually attached to the 40th chapter of the Vājasaneyi-saṃhitā[1]), *Kena*, and *C'hāndogya* (of the Sāma-veda), and *Kaṭha*, *Praśna*, *Muṇḍaka*, *Māṇḍukya* (of the Atharva-veda), *Bṛihad-āraṇyaka* (at-

[1] I was told by a great Paṇḍit that this was the only Upanishad entitled to be called *apaurusheya*, *i. e.* not written by men.

tached to the Śatapatha-brāhmaṇa), *Aitareya* (belonging to the Ṛig-veda), *Taittirīya* (belonging to the black Yajur-veda).

It is interesting to trace the rudiments of the later philosophy amid the labyrinth of mystical ideas and puerile conceits which bewilder the reader of the Upanishads. They are the link connecting the Brāhmaṇas with the Darśanas or regular philosophical systems, their connexion with the former being shown by the frequent allusions to sacrificial rites. But they rise to a far higher level than the Brāhmaṇas; and in some of them striking thoughts, original ideas, and lofty language redeem the absurdities of the mysticism.

The following literal translation of part of the Iśā Upanishad (regarded as one of the most important) will afford a good example of the pantheistic doctrines of Brāhmanism, as they first emerge in this portion of Indian sacred literature :—

Whate'er exists within this universe
Is all to be regarded as enveloped
By the great Lord, as if wrapped in a vesture.
There is one only Being who exists
Unmoved, yet moving swifter than the mind;
Who far outstrips the senses, though as gods
They strive to reach him; who himself at rest
Transcends the fleetest flight of other beings;
Who, like the air, supports all vital action.
He moves, yet moves not; he is far, yet near;
He is within this universe. Whoe'er beholds
All living creatures as in him and him—
The universal Spirit—as in all,
Henceforth regards no creature with contempt.

We now pass on to a brief notice of the actual

systems of philosophy. These are not regarded as part of Śruti or Revelation.

They are sometimes called the Shaṭ Śāstras or 'Six Instruments of True Teaching,' sometimes the Shaḍ Darśanas, or 'Six Demonstrations of Truth.' They had not shaped themselves into separate schools at the period when we may suppose the present version of Manu's law-book to have been drawn up in the fifth century B.C. As, however, the six Darśanas grew directly out of the Upanishads, and as most of their doctrines preceded, or were contemporaneous with the compilation of Manu's laws, the names of the six schools may here be enumerated.

They are,—1. The *Nyāya*, founded by Gotama. 2. The *Vaiśeshika*, by Kaṇāda. 3. The *Sāṅkhya*, by Kapila. 4. The *Yoga*, by Patanjali. 5. The *Mīmānsā*, by Jaimini. 6. The *Vedānta*, by Bādarāyaṇa or Vyāsa.

They were delivered in Sūtras or aphorisms, which are held to be the basis of all subsequent teaching under each head (see note p. 34).

The date of the composition of these aphorisms cannot be settled with certainty. Nor is it possible to decide when the six schools were finally systematized, nor which of the six preceded the other. Some of them are dualistic (affirming the co-existence of two eternal principles); some non-dualistic (insisting on the unity of all being). Their distinctive features are explained in the Appendix. Our present concern is with those lines of metaphysical speculation which preceded the formulation of distinct philosophical creeds.

It seems tolerably certain that about five or six centuries before the commencement of the Christian era, a mighty stir took place in thinking minds throughout the then civilized world. Thus, when Buddha arose in India, Greece had her great philosophical thinker in Pythagoras, Persia in Zoroaster, and China in Confucius. Men began to ask themselves earnestly such questions as—What am I? Whence have I come? Whither am I going? How can I explain my consciousness of personal existence? What is the relationship between my material and immaterial nature? What is this world in which I find myself? How can I explain the deepest mystery of nature—the history of creation? Did a wise, good, and all-powerful Being create the world out of nothing? or did it evolve itself out of an eternal germ? or did it come together by a fortuitous concurrence of eternal atoms? If created by a Being of infinite wisdom, how can I account for the inequalities of condition in it—good and evil, happiness and misery? Has the creator form, or is he formless? Has he any qualities or none?

Certainly in India no satisfactory solution of questions such as these was to be found in the prayers and hymns of the ancient Indo-Āryan poets, which, though called Veda or 'knowledge' by the Brāhmans, did not even profess to furnish any real knowledge on these points, but merely gave expression to the first gropings of the human mind, searching for truth by the uncertain light of natural phenomena.

Nor did the ritualistic Brāhmaṇas contribute anything to the elucidation of such topics. They merely encouraged the growth of a superstitious belief in the efficacy of sacrifices, and fostered the increasing dependence of the multitude on a mediatorial caste of priests, supposed to be the constituted medium of communication between men and gods. Still these momentous questions pressed for solution, and the minds of men finding no rest in mere traditional revelation, and no satisfaction in mere external rites, turned inwards, each thinker endeavouring to think out for himself the great problems of life by the aid of his own reason. Hence were composed the mystical Upanishads already described. Be it remembered that these treatises were not regarded as antagonistic to revelation, but rather as complementary of it. They were held to be an integral portion of the Veda, and even its loftiest utterance—the apex to which all previous revelation tended. Probably the simple fact was, that as it was found impossible to preclude the Kshatriyas and other inferior classes from rationalistic inquiry, the Brāhmans, with their usual astuteness, determined on making it their own, and dignifying its first development in the Upanishads with the title of Veda.

Brāhmanism and rationalistic philosophy, therefore, advanced hand in hand. Any Brāhman might become a philosopher, provided he gave a nominal assent to the Veda. But if a Kshatriya free-thinker, like Buddha, asserted that any one might be a teacher of philosophy, or might gain emancipation for himself, irrespectively of the Veda or of the Brāhmans, he was at once denounced as an infidel.

Such unbelieving free-thinkers soon became numerous in India. For, in truth, a process of action and reaction has marked the whole course of Hindūism. The heretical Buddhistic movement (more fully described in chapter vi.) was nothing but a natural reaction from the tyranny of Brāhmanism and caste. It was like the return swing of a pendulum to which an impulse was given by one great and enlightened man. It was a rebound from excessive intolerance to the broadest tolerance. It was the name for unfettered religious thought asserting itself without fear of consequences.

The orthodox schools of philosophy, on the other hand, were the homes of those rationalists who sacrificed honesty at the shrine of Brāhmanical respectability. These schools went through the form of acknowledging the authority of the Veda. Yet two at least of the six, which taught the eternal distinctness of spirit and matter, viz. the *Vaiśeshika* and *Sāṅkhya*, proceeded almost to the same length with Buddhism, even to the practical ignoring of a supreme intelligent creator.

Leaving these points to be explained more fully in the Appendix, let us briefly trace the common lines of philosophical thought growing directly out of the Upanishads. This common creed is clearly indicated in Manu's law-book, and even at the present day may be detected underlying the faith of most thinking Hindūs, to whatever sect or system they may nominally belong.

This common philosophical creed, then, asserts :—

1. The eternity of the soul, both retrospectively and prospectively.

Note that soul is regarded as of two kinds : *a.* the supreme soul (variously called *Paramātman*, *Brahman*, *Purusha*, *&c.*) ;

b. the personal individual soul of living beings, called *Jīvātman.* If any entity is eternal it can have had no beginning or it must have an end. Hence souls both supreme and individual, whether they be regarded as different or identical, have always existed and must ever exist.

2. The eternity of the matter or substance out of which the universe has been evolved.

Note that this evolution may take place, according to some materialists, from gross particles of matter; or, as in the orthodox Vedānta system, immediately from soul itself. This is a result of that fixed dogma of a Hindū philosopher's belief—*nā-vastuno vastusiddhiḥ*, ex nihilo nihil fit,—nothing can be produced out of nothing.

3. The soul, though itself abstract thought and knowledge, can only exercise thought, consciousness, sensation, and cognition, and indeed can only act and will when connected with external objects of sensation, invested with some bodily form, and joined to mind (*manas*).

For observe that mind is an internal organ of sense, a sort of inlet of thought into the soul, belonging only to the body, and quite as distinct from the soul as any external organ of the body.

4. The union of soul and body is productive of bondage, and, in the case of human souls, of misery.

For note that the soul, so united, becomes conscious of personal existence and individuality, and is capable of receiving impressions pleasurable or painful. Then it commences acting; but all action, good or bad, leads to bondage because it entails a consequence, according to the maxim *Avaśyam eva bhoktavyaṃ kṛitaṃ karma śubhāśubham*, 'When an action, good or bad, has been committed, its fruit must of necessity be eaten.' Hence if an act be good it must be rewarded, and if bad it must be punished.

5. In order to accomplish the working out of the consequences, or ripenings of acts (*karma-vipāka*), the soul must be removed to a place of reward or punishment, which reward or punishment, however, is neither full and effectual nor final.

For observe that the heavens of the Hindū system are only steps on the road to final beatitude, and the hells, though places of terrible torture,[1] are merely temporary purgatories.

The soul must leave these and return to corporeal existence, migrating into higher, intermediate, and lower forms, according to its shades of merit or demerit, and as it progresses towards emancipation from separate existence, passing through the four stages of bliss called *sālokya*, living in the same heaven with God, *sāmīpya*, nearness to God, *sārūpya*, assimilation to the likeness of God, till the great end of *sāyujya*, or complete union with the Supreme, has been attained.

6. The transmigration of the soul, through an innumerable succession of bodies,[2] is the true explanation of the existence of evil in the world.

For note that misery, disease, depravity, inequality of fortune, and diversity of character, good or bad, are simply the consequences of acts done by each soul of its own free will in former

---

[1] Twenty-one in number. See note 2 to p. 66 of 'Indian Wisdom.' (Allen & Co.)

[2] The popular theory is that every being must pass through eighty-four lakhs of births, a lakh being one hundred thousand.

bodies, which acts exert on that soul an irresistible power, very significantly called *Adṛishṭa*, because felt and 'not seen.' Hence the soul has to bear the consequences of its own actions only, being tossed hither and thither by a force set in motion by itself, but which can never be guarded against, because its operation depends on deeds committed in former lives quite beyond control, and even unremembered.

From a consideration of the above six essential elements of Brāhmanical philosophy we find that its one great aim is to teach men to abstain from action of every kind, good or bad; as much from liking as from disliking, as much from loving as from hating, and even from indifference. Actions are the fetters of the embodied soul, which when it has shaken off, it will lose all sense of individual personality and return to the condition of simple soul. This constitutes *Pramā* or true knowledge; this is the *summum bonum* of Brāhmanism; this is the only real bliss—the loss of separate identity by complete absorption (*sāyujya*) into the Supreme and only really existing Being, who is wholly unfettered by action, and without qualities of any kind (*nirguṇa*), and called *sac-cid-ānanda*,[1] because he is pure life (with nothing, however, to live for), pure thought (with nothing to think about), pure joy (with nothing to rejoice about).

[1] This is the trinity of Brāhmanical philosophy.

CHAPTER V.

BRĀHMANICAL LAW, DOMESTIC USAGES, AND CASTE.

HAVING traced the first rise and development of Brāhmanical philosophy, we shall be better prepared to enter on that phase of Brāhmanism which resulted from the growth of scepticism, viz. the substitution of social and domestic usages,—varying according to caste and tribe,—in place of public ritual and sacrifices.

Of this period, the Gṛihya-sūtras, and the Dharma-śāstras, or law-books of Manu and of Yājnavalkya, are the best exponents.

The Gṛihya-sūtras are collections of aphoristic rules, which are only distinguished from the Śrauta-sūtras of the Kalpa-Vedanga (see p. 15) because they do not relate to Śrauta or Vedic sacrifices so much as to domestic rites. The law-book of Manu, which may be assigned in its present form to about the fifth century B.C., is a metrical version of the traditional observances of a tribe of Brāhmans called Mānavas, who probably belonged to a school of the black Yajur-veda and lived in the north-west of India, not far from Delhi, which observances were originally embodied in their Gṛihya-sūtras. To these Sūtras many precepts on religion, morality, and philosophy were added by an author or authors unknown, the whole being collected in more recent times by a Brāhman or Brāhmans, who, to give weight and dignity to the collection, assigned its authorship to the mythical sage Manu.

Without attempting to determine the real authorship or to settle the exact date of the present compilation, we may safely affirm that the well-known collection of precepts commonly called 'the code of Manu' is perhaps the oldest and most sacred Sanskṛit work after the Veda and its Śrauta-sūtras. Although standing in a manner at the head of *Smṛiti*, or post-Vedic literature, it is connected with the Veda through these Sūtras, as the philosophical Darśanas are through the Upanishads. Even if not the oldest of post-Vedic writings, it is certainly the most interesting, both as presenting a picture of the usages, manners, and intellectual condition of an important part of the Hindū race at a remote period, and as revealing the exaggerated nature of the rules by which the Brāhmans sought to perpetuate an organized caste-system in subordination to themselves. At the same time, it is in other respects perhaps one of the most remarkable books that the literature of the whole world can offer, and some of its moral precepts are worthy of Christianity itself.

The compilation as now presented to us is an irregular compendium of rules which were probably in force in a particular part of India for a long period of time, and were handed down orally. It is tolerably certain that the whole of India was never under one government. Some few powerful monarchs are known to have acquired sovereignty over very extensive territories, and were then called C'akra-vartins; but we must not suppose that the term 'Code,' as applied to

Manu's law-book, is intended to denote a systematic arrangement of laws actually prevalent over the whole of such territories. In later times it became the basis of Hindū jurisprudence, but it was long before it worked its way to acceptance with the entire Hindū community; and although this law-book has now secured for itself a degree of reverence throughout the whole of India, only second to that accorded to the Veda, it was, without doubt, originally a mere local collection.

It will be found that, after eliminating the purely religious and philosophical precepts, the greater number of its rules fall under the following four heads:—

1. *Ācāra*, 'immemorial practices,' which are described as *Sad-ācāra*, 'approved practices,' sanctioned by the Veda and by Smṛiti, if they are those which prevailed between the two sacred rivers, Sarasvatī and Dṛishadvatī, in the region called Brahmāvarta. These, in fact, include all the observances of caste, regarded as constituting the highest law and highest religion.

2. *Vyavahāra*, 'practices of law and government,' embracing the procedure of legal tribunals, rules of judicature and civil and criminal law.

3. *Prāyaś-citta*, 'penitential exercises,' comprehending rules of expiation.

4. *Karma-phala*, 'consequences of acts,' especially as involving repeated births through numberless existences, until the attainment of final beatitude.

Since the precepts under these four heads were framed by men who were Brāhmans of the Mānava school, it is only natural that they should have especial reference to the life of Brāhmans, the regulations for which engross six books, and are besides introduced everywhere throughout the other six. But as the Brāhman could not be supported in his pretensions without the strong arm of the Kshatriya, or military class, a large portion of the work is devoted to the definition of the Kshatriya's duties and an exaggerated delineation of the kingly character and office; while the Vaiśyas or agriculturists, and Śudras or servants, though essential to Manu's *C'āturvarṇya* or fourfold social system, as well as the mixed classes, are little noticed. Here is an epitome of the twelve books:—

After an account of the creation of the world in the first book, the four stages of a Brāhman's life are the only subjects treated of in regular order in the second, third, fourth, fifth, and sixth books, four books being devoted to the duties of the religious student and married householder, and the sixth book treating of the last two stages of anchorite and religious mendicant.

The seventh and eighth books propound the rules of government, principally, of course, for the guidance of the second great class or Kshatriyas, from which the king was chosen. The ninth book contains precepts on the subject of women, husband and wife, their offspring and the law of inheritance and division of property, with additional rules for kings, and a few precepts relative to the two remaining principal castes. It also describes the employments to which the several classes are restricted, and states the occupations permitted to Brāhmans, Kshatriyas, Vaiśyas, and S'ūdras in times of exigency and distress. The eleventh book gives rules of expiation, both for the sins of the present life—especially sins against caste—and for the effects of offences committed in previous bodies, as shown in congenital diseases, &c. The twelfth continues the subject of the recompenses or consequences of acts, good or bad, as leading to reward in heaven or punishment in various hells, and to triple degrees of transmigration. It closes with directions as to the best means of obtaining final beatitude and absorption into the universal essence.

The simplicity of Manu's organization of classes, if it be not merely theoretical, bears witness to the great antiquity of a portion of the code. According to Book X. 3, 4, there are only four pure classes, as follow:—

The Brāhman, the Kshatriya, and the Vaiśya constitute the three twice-born classes (as receiving a second spiritual birth through investiture with the sacred thread); the S'ūdra is once-born, and constitutes the fourth class; there is no fifth class. From priority of birth, from superiority of origin (in being sprung from the mouth of the Creator), from possession of the Veda (*i.e.* from the right of repeating, teaching, and expounding it), and from a distinction in the reception of the sacrificial thread (as the most important of the twelve Sanskāras or purificatory rites) the Brāhman is the lord of all classes.

A Brāhman, whether learned or unlearned, is a mighty divinity, just as fire is a mighty divinity, whether consecrated or unconsecrated (ix. 317).

In the tenth book, however, we have a more developed social system depicted, and a number of mixed castes are described as resulting from the intermarriage of the pure classes. They have a variety of names, such as *Mūrdhāvasikta*, *Māhishya*, *Karaṇa* or *Kāya-stha*, *Ambashṭha* or *Vaidya*, *Āyogava*, *Dhigvaṇa*, *Pukkasa*, *Caṇḍāla*, and are restricted to particular occupations.

The superiority of the Brāhmans in the Hindū lawyer's scheme is the hinge on which the whole social system turns.

The Brāhmans are supposed to constitute the great central body, around which all other classes and orders of beings revolve like satellites. Not only are they invested with divine dignity, but they are bound together by the most stringent rules; while the other three classes of soldiers, agriculturists, and servants are made powerless for combined resistance by equally stringent regulations, one class being separated from the other by insurmountable barriers.

It was found indeed necessary to conciliate the Kshatriya class. The most exalted eulogies were lavished on kings; but Brāhmans were to act as their advisers, and to have much of the judicial authority and interpretation of the laws in their own hands, and were always theoretically superior in rank—a circumstance which led in the end to jealousies, feuds, and bloody contests between the first two classes. Certain privileges also naturally fell to the Vaiśyas, and both they and the Kshatriyas were equally with the Brāhmans entitled to the appellation *Dvi-ja*, 'twice born.' Their whole status, however, depended upon various domestic rites, to the due conduct of which the superintendence of Brāhmans was indispensable.

In short, the distinction of caste and the inherent superiority of one class over the three others were thought to be as much a law of nature and a matter of divine appointment as the creation of separate classes of animals, with insurmountable differences of physical constitution, such as elephants, lions, horses, and dogs.

When the increase of the Brāhmanical class compelled the secularization of many of its members, they were allowed to engage in the occupations of the other classes. Practice and theory then became very different, and in later times caste distinctions separated the Brāhmans themselves, so that separate tribes adopted separate usages. It is essential, however, that the original theory of the life of a Brāhman as laid down by Manu should be clearly understood. It may be described as follows :—

Every Brāhman had to pass through four Āśramas, or conditions of life; that is to say, his life was divided into four periods according as he became successively,—1. Unmarried student (*brahma-ćārin*); 2. Married householder (*gṛiha-stha*); 3. Anchorite (*vānaprastha*); 4. Religious devotee (*bhikshu* or *parivrājaka* or *sannyāsin*).

As unmarried student the young Brāhman was to reside with his preceptor until he had gained a thorough knowledge of the three Vedas. He was to go through twelve Sanskāras or 'purificatory rites,' which purify a man from the taint of sin derived from his parents, and are enjoined with certain variations on all the three first classes alike. They are as follow :—

1. *Garbhādhāna* or *garbha-lambhana*, 'ceremony on conception'; 2. *Punsavana*, on the first indication of a living male's conception; 3. *Sīmantonnayana*, arranging the parting of the mother's hair in the fourth, sixth, or eighth month of pregnancy; 4. *Jāta-karman*, touching an infant's tongue with honey and *ghī* thrice at birth; 5. *Nāma-karaṇa*, giving a name on the tenth or twelfth day after birth; 6. *Nishkramaṇa*, taking out the child in the fourth month to see the sun; 7. *Anna-prāśana*, feeding it with rice between the fifth and eighth month; 8. *C'ūḍākarman*, or *ćaula*, tonsure of the hair, except one lock, on the crown of the head, in the third year; 9. *Upanayana*, induction into the order of a twice-born man by investiture with the sacred cord; 10. *Keśānta*, cutting off the hair, performed on a Brāhman in his sixteenth year, on a Kshatriya in his twenty-second, on a Vaiśya in his twenty-fourth; 11. *Samāvartana*, solemn return home after completing a course

of study with a preceptor; 12. *Vivāha*, marriage, which completes the purification and regeneration of the twice-born.

Of the above rites—1, 2, 3, and 10, are little observed. The other eight are more worthy of attention; 8 and 9 are of considerable legal importance even in the present day, and 7 is still practised; 7 and 12 are said to be the only rites allowed to Śūdras, and the 12th, *Vivāha*, 'marriage,' is a religious duty incumbent on all persons alike.

Other Sanskāras practised in some parts of India, are mentioned, such as *Karṇa-vedha*, 'boring the ears'; and occasionally the imparting of the Sāvitrī or sacred Vedic text, commonly called Gāyatrī, which ought to be performed at *Upanayana*, is reserved for a separate ceremony four days later.

One of the most important of the above Sanskāras is certainly *Upanayana*, induction into the order of a twice-born man by investiture with the sacred cord.' This rite is enjoined for a Brāhman in his eighth year, for a Kshatriya in his eleventh, and for a Vaiśya in his twelfth, though the time may be extended in each case.

The sacred cord, which is generally a thin coil of three threads, commonly called *Yajnopavīta*, is worn over the left shoulder, and allowed to hang down diagonally across the body to the right hip. The wearing of it by the three twice-born classes is the mark of their second spiritual birth. There was some difference in the kind of thread worn, according to the class of the wearer, thus:

The sacred cord of a Brāhman must be of cotton so as to be put on over his head in a coil of three threads; that of a Kshatriya, of hemp; that of a Vaiśya, of wool.

The ceremony of induction begins by the youth's

standing opposite the sun, and walking thrice round the fire. The Guru then consecrates the Yajnopavīta by repeating the Gāyatrī ten times. Then, girt with the thread, the youth asks alms from the assembled company, to indicate that he undertakes to provide himself and his preceptor with food. The Guru then initiates him into the daily use of the sacred Sāvitrī prayer (called Gāyatrī, because it is in the three-measured Gāyatrī metre), preceded by three suppressions of breath, the triliteral syllable *Om* and the three Vyāhṛitis, or mystical words, *Bhūr*, *Bhuvaḥ*, *Svar*, and admits him to the privilege of repeating the three Vedas, and of performing other religious rites, none of which are allowed before investiture. The Gāyatrī prayer (Ṛig-veda, iii. 62, 10) may be thus translated :—

Let us meditate (or, we meditate) on that excellent glory of the divine Vivifier. May he enlighten (or stimulate) our understandings. [*Tat savitur vareṇyam bhargo devasya dhīmahi, dhiyo yo naḥ praćodayāt.*]

This prayer is repeated, or muttered, with the aid of a rosary[1] (*japa-mālā*) five, ten, twenty-eight, or even one hundred and eight times at the two Sandhyās of sunrise and sunset; and those who aim at great sanctity repeat it at the three Sandhyās, or divisions of the day, sunrise, noon, and sunset. The right of investiture is concluded by the binding on of a girdle (*mekhalā*), made of Munja grass.

---

[1] According to whether a man is a Vaishṇava or S'aiva, rosaries made either of Tulasī wood or Rudrāksha berries are employed. The Vaishṇava rosaries contain 108 beads, while the S'aiva have either 32 Rudrāksha berries or that number doubled.

The young Brāhman is then a *Brahma-ćārī*, or unmarried bachelor, and is supposed to reside with his preceptor till he has acquired a knowledge of the Veda. He is every day to bathe; to offer oblations of water to the gods, holy sages, and departed ancestors; and to feed the sacred fire with fuel. But he is forbidden to perform the regular Śrāddha offerings to deceased persons till his studentship is completed. He is to abstain from meat, perfumes, unguents, sensuality, wrath, covetousness, dancing, music, gambling, detraction of others, falsehood, impurity of all kinds, and is never to injure any being. At the end of his studentship the young Brāhman is to perform the proper Sanskāra ceremony called *Samāvartana* with the prescribed ablutions (*snāna*) on the occasion of his solemn return to his own home;[1] soon after which he is obliged to take a wife and to become a householder (*Gṛihastha*). As to marriage, the following directions are given by Manu:—

Eight forms of marriage are enumerated, viz., *Brāhma*, *Daiva*, *Ārsha*, *Prājāpatya*, *Āsura*, *Gāndharva*, *Rākshasa*, and *Paiśāća*. Of these, the first four are the most approved for a Brāhman, but the first is practically the only one now in use. The Gāndharva marriage ('from affection without any nuptial rite'), and Rākshasa ('marrying a girl carried off as a prize in war') were allowable for Kshatriyas; the Āsura and Paiśāća were prohibited.

In modern times marriage ceremonies last for several days,

---

[1] In the present day the residence of the young Brāhman with a preceptor is not enforced, so that the ceremonies of Upanayana and Samāvartana are made to succeed each other within a day or two, or may even take place on the same day.

and are accompanied with great festivities. They cannot be commenced till the *Jyotishī*, or family astrologer, has fixed the auspicious day and hour. The bride is given away by her father or his representative at her own home. Perhaps the most important parts of the ceremony are the Saptapadī[1] or the leading of the bride three times round the sacred fire—each time in seven steps—the offering of the burnt oblation (*homa*) by the bridegroom, the binding together of the bride and bridegroom by a cord passed round their necks, and the tying together of their dresses. The rite is of course commenced by the worship of the god Gaṇeśa, who wards off the obstacles by which all undertakings are liable to be thwarted through the malice of evil demons.

After marriage, which, as we have already seen, is one of the twelve Sanskāras, and a religious duty incumbent on all, the married Brāhman is to perform every day all the domestic duties of a householder, and especially the five Mahā-yajnas, or great acts of worship;' viz.:—

1. *Brahma-yajna*, 'worship of Brahman,' performed by repetition of the Veda; 2. *Pitṛi-yajna*, 'worship of departed ancestors' by daily offerings of water and by periodical S'rāddha ceremonies; 3. *Deva-yajna*, 'worship of the gods' by morning and evening oblations in fire, &c.; 4. *Bhūta-yajna*, 'worship of all beings,' including good and evil spirits, animals, &c., by scattering rice grains, &c., on the ground outside the door for animals to devour;[2] 5. *Manushya-yajna*, 'worship of men,' performed by hospitality to guests.

Some of these must be regularly performed at the three Sandhyās, or at sunrise, mid-day, and sunset.

---

[1] See 'Indian Wisdom,' p. 199.

[2] This offering is called *bali*, and is made with a particular mantra, part of which is as follows: 'Om to the Viśvadevas, to the universal gods, to men, beasts, birds, reptiles, the

In all Hindū systems diet is a most important subject, for food is supposed not only to affect the blood, but the whole character, moral and religious. The food a man eats must be ceremonially (not chemically) pure, or he instantly becomes degraded. This doctrine has been carried to such a point in modern times, that the preservation of caste depends in great part on strict adherence to the rules laid down on the subject of food, its preparation, and the persons in whose company it is eaten (see chap. xi.). Manu's chief directions are as follow:—

The eating of flesh and of fish[1] by twice-born men is, as a general rule, prohibited, the drinking of spirituous liquor is included among the five great sins (the other four being the killing of a Brāhman, stealing gold from a Brāhman, adultery with the wife of a religious teacher, and association with any one guilty of these crimes), and many other kinds of food, such as garlic, onions, leeks, mushrooms, and carnivorous birds are forbidden. But it is a proof of the antiquity of Manu's code that it permits the eating of meat, and even the drinking of wine on certain solemn occasions (Manu, v. 56), and that it directs flesh meat to be eaten at particular S'rāddhas (iii. 12, 3; iv. 131).

With regard to the householder's wife and the condition of women as depicted by Manu, we may observe that their position is one of entire subordination,

---

Siddhas, the Yakshas, the Daityas, Pretas, Piśāćas, trees, and whoever desires to have food receive this *bali* from me. Om, may the ants, worms, insects, and whoever are hungry, being imprisoned in corporeal frames, receive this food offered by me. Om to the Bhūtas and all beings, be satisfied with the *bali* scattered by me. Om to the crows, to the twin dogs, S'yāma and S'avala, to the dogs, to the Ćaṇḍālas, &c.

[1] Some tribes of Brāhmans are now permitted to eat fish.

amounting in theory to a complete abnegation of what in these days would be called 'women's rights.'

A Brahman who has been in succession a *Brahma-ćārī* and *Gṛihastha* ought properly to pass through two other stages of existence as a *Vānaprastha* or hermit, and as a *Bhikshu* or *Sannyāsin; i.e.* a religious devotee who has given up all worldly connections. But these are not now obligatory.

As to death, the filial piety of the Hindūs is notably manifested in the importance attached to funeral rites and to Śrāddhas. These must be distinguished from each other. Funeral rites (*antyeshṭi*) are *amangala*, 'inauspicious,' while Śrāddhas are *mangala*, 'auspicious.' To understand this it should be borne in mind that when a man dies, his *sthūla-sarīra*, or 'gross body,' is burned[1] (this being in fact the *antyā ishṭi*, last sacrifice offered in fire), but his soul cannot quit the gross body without a vehicle of some kind. This vehicle is the *linga-śarīra* or 'subtile body,' sometimes described as *angushṭha-mātra*, 'of the size of a thumb,' invested in which the deceased man remains hovering near the burning-ground. He is then in the condition of a simple individual soul invested with a subtile body, and is called a *preta*, *i.e.* a departed spirit or ghost. He has no real body capable of enjoying or suffering anything, and is consequently in a restless, uncomfortable plight. Moreover, while in this condition he is held to be an

[1] Infants under two years old, however, must be buried, not burnt.—See 'Indian Wisdom,' p. 302. Great ascetics (Sannyāsīs) and holy men (Sādhus) are also generally buried, and their tombs called Samādhis.

impure being, and all the relations who celebrate his funeral rites are held to be impure also until the first Śrāddha is performed. Furthermore, if he dies away from his kindred, who alone can perform the funeral ceremonies, and who are perhaps unaware of his death, and unable therefore to perform them, he becomes a *piśāća*, or foul wandering ghost, disposed to take revenge for its misery upon all living creatures by a variety of malignant acts.

The object, then, of the *antyeshṭi*, or funeral rites, which are celebrated for ten days after death, is not only to soothe or give *śānti* by libations of consecrated water to the troubled spirit, but to furnish the *preta* with an intermediate body, between the *linga* or 'subtile' and the *sthūla* or 'gross body'—with a body, that is to say, which is capable of enjoying or suffering, and which is composed of gross particles, though not of the same kind as the earthly gross body.

In this manner only can the *preta* obtain *gati*, or 'progress' onward, either through the temporary heaven, or else through the temporary hells (which as we have seen are not places of eternal punishment but merely purgatories) to other births and ultimate emancipation. The following is a brief account of the more modern funeral ceremonies and subsequent Śrāddhas.

On the first day after death a *piṇḍa*, or round ball (generally of some kind of flour or of rice and milk), is offered with libations of water, &c., on which the *preta* is supposed to feed, and which endows it with the rudiment or basis of the requisite body, whatever that basis may be. Next day another *piṇḍa* is offered with water, &c., which gives it, perhaps, limbs, such as arms and legs. Then it receives hands, feet, &c. This goes on for ten days, and the offering of the *piṇḍa* on the tenth day gives the head. No sooner does the *preta* obtain a complete body than it becomes a *pitṛi*, when, instead of being regarded as impure, it is held to be a *deva*, or 'deity,' and practically worshipped as such in the *śrāddha* ceremonies, the first of which takes place on the 11th day after death. Hence, a śrāddha is not a funeral ceremony, but a *pitṛi-yajna*, or worship of departed ancestors, which worship, however, is something different from *pūjā* to a god. It is performed by making offerings of round balls of rice, flour, &c., with accompaniments of sacred grass, flowers, and-sprinklings of water, and with repetitions of mantras and texts from the Sāma-veda, the whole ceremonial being conducted, not in a temple, but at any sacred spot, such as the margin of a river, or even in private houses. The ceremony is continued at stated periods with a view to accelerate the *gati* or 'progress' of the *pitṛis* onwards to heaven, and then through the various stages of bliss before described (see p. 51). The efficacy of *S'rāddhas*, performed at Gayā (see pp. 176, 177), is this, that wherever in this progress onwards departed relatives may have arrived, the S'rāddhas take them at once to Vaikuṇṭha, or Vishṇu's heaven.

The departed relatives especially entitled to benefit by the Śrāddha rites are as follows :—

1. Father, grandfather, great grandfather; 2. Mother, mother's father and grandfather; 3. Stepmother, if any; 4. Father's mother, grandmother, and great grandmother; 5. Father's brothers; 6. Mother's brothers; 7. Father's sisters; 8. Mother's sisters; 9. Sisters and brothers; 10. Fathers-in-law. An eleventh person is sometimes added, viz. the family spiritual teacher (*guru*).

Śrāddhas are of various kinds, and performed at various times, such as *Nitya*, regular; *Pārvaṇa*, at particular changes of the moon; *Ekoddishṭa*, on special occasions and with reference to particular persons. These ceremonies with those at birth (see p. 59) and death, at investiture with the sacred thread (*upanayana*) and marriage (*vivāha*) already described, constitute in the present day the most important religious rites among the Hindūs.

Some Śrāddhas—especially those first performed after the termination of the funeral rites—are accompanied with much feasting and costly gifts to the Brāhmans invited to assist at their celebration, and some are actually commuted for this feeding and feasting of Brāhmans.[1]

The performance of the first Śrāddha is more particularly marked by largesses of all kinds, and sometimes, it is said, costs a rich man a sum equivalent to several thousand pounds. It should take place on the eleventh day, or the day after mourning expires, and then at least once a month for twelve successive months, this monthly (*māsika*) ceremony being called by Manu *Anvāhārya*. Afterwards it must be performed annually (*Sāṃvatsarika*) on all anniversaries of a father's death. The following should be noted :—

The offering of the Piṇḍa, or ball of rice, &c., to deceased fathers at a S'rāddha is of great importance in regard to the Hindū law of inheritance. It furnishes the principal evidence of kinship, on which the title to participate in the patrimony is founded, no power of making wills being recognized in Manu, or any other authoritative code of Hindū jurisprudence. The

---

[1] Many S'rāddhas certainly appear to have more reference to the living than to the dead, and others seem to be performed by a process of feeding and feeing Brāhmans (*Brahmaṇa-santarpaṇa*), who are supposed to represent the Pitṛis. Some of these are called *Hasta-śrāddha*, *Hiraṇya-śrāddha*, *Amānna-śrāddha*, *Dadhi-śrāddha*, *Nāndī-śrāddha*. The last is a homage paid to ancestors before performing such joyous ceremonies as marriage, investiture with the sacred thread (*upanayana*), and birth ceremonies.

Gotra, or family, is in fact a corporate body bound together by what may be called *Sapiṇḍa*ship and *Samānodaka*ship. All who offer the ball of rice (*piṇḍa*) and water (*udaka*) together are *Sapiṇḍas* and *Samānodakas* to each other, and a kind of intercommunication and interdependence is thus continually maintained between the dead and living members of a family, extending to three generations on both sides.

As regards transmigration, Manu declares that the triple order of the passage of the soul through the highest, middle, and lowest stages of existence results from good or bad acts, words, and thoughts produced by the influence of the three Guṇas, *Sattva*, *Rajas*, and *Tamas* (see p. 194 of the Appendix); and that for sins of act, a man takes a vegetable or mineral form; for sins of word, the form of a bird or beast; for sins of thought, that of a man of the lowest caste. A triple self-command in thought, word, and deed leads to emancipation from all births, and final beatitude.

A few specimens of Manu's moral precepts are here subjoined :—

Daily perform thine own appointed work
Unweariedly ; and to obtain a friend—
A sure companion to the future world—
Collect a store of virtue like the ants
Who garner up their treasures into heaps ;
For neither father, mother, wife, nor son,
Nor kinsman, will remain beside thee then,
When thou art passing to that other home—
Thy virtue will thy only comrade be (iv. 238, 239).

Single is every living creature born,
Single he passes to another world,
Single he eats the fruits of evil deeds,
Single, the fruit of good ; and when he leaves
His body like a log or heap of clay
Upon the ground, his kinsmen walk away ;

Virtue alone stays by him at the tomb,
And bears him through the dreary trackless gloom
(iv. 240, 242).

Depend not on another, rather lean
Upon thyself; trust to thine own exertions.
Subjection to another's will gives pain;
True happiness consists in self-reliance (iv. 160).

Strive to complete the task thou hast commenced;
Wearied, renew thy efforts once again;
Again fatigued, once more the work begin;
So shalt thou earn success and fortune win (ix. 300)

There are at least nineteen other well-known codes[1] besides that of Manu. Of these the best-known is that of *Yājnavalkya*, which, with its most celebrated commentary the *Mitāksharā* by *Vijnāneśvara*, is now the principal authority of the School of Benares and Middle India. It seems originally to have emanated from a school of the White *Yajur-veda* in Mithilā or North Behar, just as we have seen that the code of the Mānanvas did from a school of the Black Yajur-veda. Book i. 2 makes the author say:—

The chief of devout sages (Yājnavalkya), dwelling in Mithilā, having reflected for a moment, said to the Munis, 'Listen to the laws which prevail in the country where the black antelope is found.' (cf. Manu, ii. 23.)

The following may be noted concerning Yājnavalkya's work:—

It is much more concise than that of Manu, being all comprised in three books instead of twelve, which circumstance leads to the inference that it has suffered even more curtailment at the hands of successive revisers of the original text than the Code of the Mānavas. Like that code it seems to have been preceded by a Vṛiddha and a Vṛihat version, and like that code,

[1] See 'Indian Wisdom,' p. 211, 304.

the whole work, as we now possess it, is written in the ordinary S loka metre. The first book is chiefly on social and caste duties (*āćāra*); the second is mainly on administrative judicature and civil and criminal law (*vyavahāra*); the third is principally on devotion, purification, expiation, penance (*prāyaś-ćitta*), &c. The Mitāksharā commentary follows the same arrangement, and is divided also into three parts.

Although Yājnavalkya's code must have represented the customs and practices prevalent in a district (Mithilā) situated in a more easterly part of India, yet nearly every precept in the first book, and a great many in the second and third, have their parallels in similar precepts occurring throughout the code of the Mānavas.

Nevertheless, it represents a later stage of Hindū development. Its arrangement is much more systematic. It presents fewer repetitions and inconsistencies, and less confusion of religion, morality, and philosophy, with civil and criminal law. As to the date of Yājnavalkya's law-book, it has been conjecturally placed in the middle of the first century of our era. The period of its first compilation cannot, of course, be fixed with certainty, but internal evidence clearly indicates that the present redaction is much more recent than that of Manu's law-book.

Two verses from Yājnavalkya's code literally translated are here subjoined as specimens :—

The success of every action depends on destiny and on a man's own effort; but destiny is evidently nothing but (the result) of a man's act in a former state of existence (i. 348; cf. Manu, vii. 205).

Some expect the whole result from destiny or from the inherent nature (or force of a thing); some expect it from the lapse of time; and some from a man's own effort; other persons of wiser judgment expect it from a combination of all these (i. 349).

CHAPTER VI.

THE BUDDHISTIC MOVEMENT, AND ITS INFLUENCE ON BRĀHMANISM.

A BRIEF account of the contact and conflict of Buddhism with Brāhmanism, and of the introduction of Buddhistic ideas into the religious creed of the Brāhmans, is essential to an accurate delineation of Hindūism. And here we are able to feel that—chronologically at least—we are not groping our way through a region of mere conjecture. We seem at last to have planted our feet on a firmer standpoint. Our story assumes more of the character of history. The date usually fixed for Buddha's death is 543 B.C. Whether this precise year for one of the greatest epochs in the religious history of the human race can be accepted is doubtful, but it is tolerably certain that Buddhism arose in Behar and Eastern Hindūstān about five centuries B.C., and that it spread with great rapidity, not by force of arms, or coercion of any kind, like Muhammadanism, but by the sheer persuasiveness of its doctrines.

The first tolerably trustworthy date in Indian history is the era of C'andra-gupta (=Sandrokottus [1])

[1] The minister of C'andra-gupta was the celebrated and crafty Brāhman C'āṇakya, the author of many well-known precepts of government and polity. In the political drama

the founder of the Maurya dynasty, who, after making himself master of Pāṭaliputra (Palibothra, Patna) and the kingdom of Magadha (Behar), extended his dominion over all Hindūstān, and presented a determined front towards Alexander's successor Seleukos Nikator, the date of the commencement of whose reign was about 312 B.C. When the latter contemplated invading India from his kingdom of Bactria, so effectual was the resistance offered by C'andra-gupta that the Greek thought it politic to form an alliance with the Hindū king, and sent his own countryman Megasthenes as an ambassador to reside at his court.

To this circumstance we owe the first authentic account of Indian manners, customs, and religious usages by an intelligent observer who was not a native, and this narrative of Megasthenes, preserved by Strabo, furnishes a basis on which we may found a fair inference that Brāhmanism and Buddhism existed side by side in India on amicable terms in the fourth century B.C. There is even ground for believing that King C'andra-gupta himself was in secret a Buddhist, though in public he paid homage to the gods of the Brāhmans; at any rate, there can be little doubt that his successor Aśoka did for Buddhism what Constantine did for Christianity—gave an impetus to its progress by adopting it as his own creed. Buddhism, then, became the state religion, the national faith of the whole kingdom of

called Mudrā-rākshasa, 'Signet-ring Rākshasa,' he is represented as having effected the death of King Nanda and secured the accession of C'andra-gupta to the throne.

Magadha, and therefore of a great portion of India.

This Aśoka is by some regarded as identical with C'andra-gupta; at any rate, their characters and much of their history are similar. He is probably the same as King Priyadarśi, whose edicts on stone pillars enjoining *Dharma*, or the practice of virtue and universal benevolence, are scattered over India from Katak in the east and Gujarāt in the west to Allahābād, Delhi, and Afghānistān on the north-west.

What then is Buddhism? It is certainly not Brāhmanism, yet it arose out of Brāhmanism, and from the first had much in common with it. Brāhmanism and Buddhism are closely interwoven with each other, yet they are very different from each other. Brāhmanism is a religion which may be described as all theology, for it makes God everything, and everything God. Buddhism is no religion at all, and certainly no theology, but rather a system of duty, morality, and benevolence, without real deity, prayer, or priest.

The name Buddha is simply an epithet meaning 'the perfectly enlightened one,' or rather one who, by perfect knowledge of the truth, is liberated from all existence, and who, before his own attainment of Nirvāṇa, or 'extinction,' reveals to the world the method of obtaining it.

The Buddha with whom we are concerned was only the last of a series of Buddhas who had appeared in previous cycles of the universe.

He was born at *Kapila-vastu*, a city and kingdom at the foot of the mountains of Nepāl, his father *S'uddhodana* being the king of that country, and his mother *Māyā-devī* being the daughter of King *Suprabuddha.* Hence he belonged to the Kshatriya class, and the name of his tribe was Śākya, while his name of Gautama (or Gotama) was that of his family. He is said to have arrived at supreme knowledge under the Bodhi tree, or 'tree of wisdom'[1] (familiarly called 'the Bo tree'), at Gayā, in Behar (Magadha). The year 588 B.C., usually given for this event, cannot be trusted. He probably commenced propagating the new faith at Benares about 500 B.C.

We have already pointed out that Buddhism was a protest against the tyranny of Brāhmanism and caste. According to the Buddha, all men are equal. All men, too, he taught, must suffer in their own persons either in the present life, or in future lives, the consequences of their own acts. All atoning sacrifice, therefore, became meaningless and useless. The penalty of sin could not be transferred to another—it could only be borne by the sinner himself, just as the reward of virtue could only be enjoyed by the virtuous man himself. To this end men might be degraded to the condition of the lower animals, of insects, and even inanimate objects, or they might rise in the scale of being, and thus expiate or be recompensed for their acts. Hence, of course, all infliction of suffering on animals was prohibited. In the edicts of Aśoka the

[1] This tree—a Pīpal—still exists behind the old Buddhist temple near Gayā; or, rather, a tree which is said to be the actual tree is perpetuated there by constantly planting new trees in the decayed stem of the old. I saw the tree myself in the beginning of 1876. Some of the Burmese Buddhists who had come to greet the Prince of Wales, were then meditating under the tree.

greatest tenderness towards them was enjoined, even to their medical treatment, if sick or diseased.

Moreover, as actions, good or bad, lead to repeated existences, the great end and object of every man was to attain non-existence (*nirvāṇa*) by self-mortification, austerity (*tapas*), and the suppression of all action.

Here, then, we have five marked features of Buddhism: 1. disregard of all caste distinctions; 2. abolition of animal sacrifice and of vicarious suffering; 3. great stress laid on the doctrine of transmigration; 4. great importance assigned to self-mortification, austerity, and abstract meditation, as an aid to the suppression of all action; 5. concentration of all human desires on the absolute extinction of all being.

There is still a sixth, which is perhaps the most noteworthy of all; viz. that the Buddha recognized no supreme deity. The only god, he affirmed, is what man himself can become.

A Buddhist, therefore, never really prays, he only meditates on the perfections of the Buddha and the hope of attaining Nirvāṇa; though practically he is subject to an all-powerful god—a god to be got rid of as soon as possible—in *Karman* 'act.'

Nor can he have any theological creed. His only confession of faith is, 'I have recourse to' (or 'place my trust in') 'Buddha, Dharma, and Sangha'—to the Buddha, the Law, and the Congregation of Priests. These three are sometimes called the three gems, and constitute a sort of Buddhistic trinity.

With regard to Sangha and Dharma we may remark that convocations or assemblies of priests or monks seem to have been common in early Buddhism.

It is said that three synods, or conferences, were held after the Buddha's death, to settle the sacred canon of scripture, which was afterwards comprised in three collections called the *Tri-piṭaka* or 'three baskets,' consisting of: 1. *Sūtra*, the discourses of the Buddha; 2. *Dharma*, the duties of the masses of the people (sometimes called *Abhi-dharma*, though this term should be restricted to the philosophical doctrines taught as a supplement to Dharma); 3. *Vinaya*, rules of discipline for the priests.

To enter upon a detailed description of the Buddhist Dharma is not part of our plan. We must confine ourselves to the briefest possible summary of its doctrines and precepts.

Four great truths are supposed to have been revealed to Buddha as the first result of his long period of abstract meditation. These together constitute what is commonly called the 'Law or doctrine of the Wheel.' They are:—

1. Suffering exists wherever there is life. 2. Suffering is caused by desire. 3. Release from suffering depends on the suppression of desire and extinction of being (*nirvāṇ* . 4. Nirvāṇa can only be obtained by following the paths pointed out by the Buddha of the period, who has achieved supreme knowledge in each cycle of the universe and who reveals to the world the method of obtaining it. These paths are eight in number, four of them, viz. right vision, right thoughts, right words, and right actions, being applicable to all men; the other four being reserved for ascetics only.

These others are right living as a recluse, right application to the study of the law, right memory in recollecting the law, and right meditation.

Hence, it is clear, that the Buddha regarded men

as divided into two classes; the first, who are still attached to a worldly life, are called *Upāsakas* or 'laymen.' The second, who by self-mortification are bent on being delivered from it, are called *S'ramaṇas*, 'ascetics,' or 'priests,' and, if they wander from place to place, *Bhikshus* or *Parivrājakas*, 'religious mendicants.' They are only priests in the sense of being teachers. Of priests in the strict sense the Buddhist religion has none; for where there is no god, there can be no need of propitiation, or even of prayer, though a short form of words is repeated, or written down and turned in a wheel,[1] as a kind of charm against diseases and malignant demons, and as having, like other acts, a kind of mechanical efficacy. Both classes of men—laymen and ascetics—must equally practise *Dharma*, 'virtue,' to avoid greater misery, either in future births, or in one of the 136 hells; for the passing through repeated births, even in the most degraded forms of life, is not sufficient punishment for the effacement of demerit, without the endurance of terrific torments in numerous hells. There are ten negative prohibitions, and eighteen positive injunctions. Of the prohibitions five are for all; viz., Kill not. Steal not. Commit no adultery. Lie not. Drink no strong drink.

The other five are for ascetics or priests; viz., Eat no food, except at stated times. Abstain from dances, theatres, songs, and music. Use no ornaments or perfumes. Use no luxurious beds. Receive no gold nor silver.

---

[1] The form is *Om maṇipadme hūm*, 'Om! the jewel in the lotus! Amen!' Or else *Amitāya Om*, 'Om! to the immeasurable One.'

Of the eighteen positive injunctions there are six perfections of conduct (*Pāramitās*)[1] incumbent on all, viz :—

1. Charity or benevolence (*dāna*). 2. Virtue or moral goodness (*śīla*). 3. Patience and forbearance (*kshānti*). 4. Fortitude (*vīrya*). 5. Meditation (*dhyāna*). 6. Knowledge (*prajnā*). Of these that which especially characterizes Buddhism is the perfection of benevolence displayed towards all living beings.

Even self-sacrifice for the good of animals and inferior creatures of all kinds is a duty.

It is recorded of the Buddha himself, that in former existences he frequently gave himself up as a substituted victim in the place of doves and other innocent creatures, to satisfy the appetites of hawks and beasts of prey; and on one occasion meeting with a famished tigress unable to feed her cubs, he was so overcome with compassion that he sacrificed his own body to supply the starving family with food.

Besides these six positive injunctions for all, there are twelve others incumbent on ascetics, viz. :—

1. To dress only in coats of rags. 2. To have a coat in three pieces sewn together with the owner's own hands. 3. To cover the coat of rags with a yellow cloak. 4. To eat only one meal daily. 5. Never to eat after noon. 6. To live only on food collected from door to door in a wooden bowl. 7. To live for part of the year in woods and jungles. 8. To have no other shelter but the leaves of trees. 9. To have no other furniture but a carpet. 10. To sit, and not to lie down, on this carpet during sleep. 11. To sit with no other support than the trunk of a tree. 12. To frequent cemeteries and burning-grounds every month for meditation on the vanity of life.

---

[1] Leading to the shore of Nirvāṇa.

These rules of conduct include many secondary precepts; for instance, not only is untruthfulness prohibited, but all bad language; not only is patience enjoined, but the bearing of injuries, resignation under misfortune, humility, repentance, and confession of sin to one another. This last was required to be practised by all priests or ascetics twice a month, and, it is said, that King Aśoka enjoined on his subjects a great quinquennial expiatory ceremony for the practice of confession and almsgiving.[1]

There remains the question—what has been the probable influence of the Buddhistic movement on Brāhmanism? The answer is—Brāhmanism has taken from Buddhism the abolition of sacrifices, great tenderness towards animal life, great intensity of belief in the doctrine of transmigration, and in the efficacy of *tapas* or self-mortification as a source of power in accelerating progress towards final emancipation.[2]

It has even received from Buddhism a tendency to recognize caste as an evil, or at least as an imperfection to be got rid of under certain circumstances and on certain occasions. It is an admitted fact that,

---

[1] One of these great ceremonies was witnessed by the Chinese pilgrim and traveller, Hiouen Thsang, at Nālandā. See Wheeler's 'History of India,' vol. iii. p. 275. (See also the Rev. J. Robson's 'Hinduism, and its Relations to Christianity.')

[2] Hindūism has borrowed ideas from Buddhism in many minor points, such as the veneration for the footprints of divine and holy personages. Notably, too, it has fixed its Tīrthas at many places held sacred by the Buddhists, such as Gayā.

although caste in the end has always reasserted itself, various Vaishṇava and Śaiva reformers [1] and founders of sects, have imitated Buddha in requiring their followers to drop caste-distinctions; and it is well known that at the meetings of *Śāktas* or *Tāntrikas*, (see p. 122) and at certain sacred places of pilgrimage (such as Purī in Orissa, and Tripati), caste, so far at least as the eating of food is concerned, is for a time entirely laid aside.[2] In short, Brāhmanism and Buddhism appear to have blended, or as it were, melted into each other, after each had reciprocally parted with something, and each had imparted something. At any rate it may be questioned whether Buddhism was ever forcibly expelled from any part of India by direct persecution, except, perhaps, in a few isolated centres of Brāhmanical fanaticism, such as the neighbourhood of Benares. Even in Benares the Chinese traveller Hiouen Thsang, found Brāhmanism and Buddhism flourishing amicably side by side in the 7th century of our era.[3] In the South of India the Buddha's doctrines seem to have met with acceptance at an early date; and Ceylon was probably converted as

---

[1] The Lingaits of the South of India have theoretically no caste among themselves. They say we all belong to a fifth caste. The same may be said of the Vaishṇavas of Bengal, followers of Ćaitanya, of various orders of ascetics and other sects. See Chapter X.

[2] In some parts of India the very name for caste is *Bhram*, 'error,' and the temple of Jagannāth is a temple of Concord for all castes.

[3] At Ellora the three series of Buddhistic, Brāhmanical, and Jain caves all run into each other, as if they co-existed.

early as B.C. 240, soon after the third Buddhist council held under King Aśoka. In other parts of India there was probably a period of Brāhmanical hostility, and perhaps of occasional persecution; but eventually Buddhism was taken by the hand, and drawn back into the Brāhmanical system by the Brāhmans themselves who met it halfway, and ended by boldly adopting the Buddha as an incarnation of Vishṇu. This has always been the astute policy of the Brāhmans of India. They have perceived the power of compromise, and overcome opposition by wise concessions and partial adaptations. It is thus that they have always enticed dissenters back to their caste-system It was thus that they became Buddhists to the Buddhists that they might win the Buddhists. Only a small section of the Buddhist community resisted all conciliation, and these are probably represented by the present sect of Jains (see p. 221 of the Appendix).

Be the actual state of the case as it may, nothing can be clearer than the fact that Buddhism has disappeared from India (the island of Ceylon being excepted), and that it has not done so without having largely contributed towards the moulding of Brāhmanism into the Hindūism of the present day.

CHAPTER VII.

DEVELOPMENT OF HINDŪISM AND THE DOCTRINE OF TRIPLE MANIFESTATION (*Tri-mūrti*).

THE period marked by the disappearance of Buddhism out of India is sometimes called the 'Revival of Brāhmanism.' If this term be adopted, then Śankarāćārya, one of the strictest and most learned of Brāhmāns, and a noted philosopher who flourished in the South of India about the end of the seventh or beginning of the eighth century,[1] ought to be called the great Revivalist preacher. Brāhmanism, however, never revived in its purity, and long before the time of Śankara had degenerated. The term Brāhmanism is more properly restricted to the purely pantheistic and not necessarily idolatrous system evolved by the Brāhmans out of the half-monotheistic, half-pantheistic religion of the Veda.

This system which was fully developed in the Vedānta philosophy, and is commonly called *Advaita* Non-dualism, insists, as we have seen, on the unity of all being.

But it has also other characteristics. It may be described as in one sense the most self-annihilating

---

[1] He is said to have revived the worship of S'iva, and is described by some as an incarnation of S'iva. Others deny his preference for the god S'iva, and make him out to have been rather a Vaishṇava in his religious proclivities.

system in the world, for it asserts that there can be no real *self* (*ātman*) existing separately from the one self-existent Supreme Self, sometimes called *Paramātman*, sometimes *Brahman*, and that when by the act of that Self the individuated spirits of men are allowed for a time an apparent separate existence, the aim of such spirits should be to be blended once more with the one Eternal Self in entire self-annihilation. A Brāhman who holds this doctrine thinks the religion of the Christian, who is conscious of severance from God, and yearns for reunion with Him, and yet does not wish his own self-consciousness to be merged in God, a very selfish kind of creed, compared with his own. It is evident, however, that there may be more real selfishness in the self-annihilating creed. For whatever may be said about the bliss of complete union (*sāyujya*) with the Supreme Spirit, the true aim of Brāhmanism, pure and simple, is not so much extinction of self, as extinction of personal existence for the sake of release from the troubles of life, and from the consequences of activity.

The term Hindūism, on the other hand, best expresses Brāhmanism after it had degenerated—to wit, that complicated system of polytheistic doctrines and caste-usages which has gradually resulted out of the mixture of Brāhmanism and Buddhism, with the non-Āryan creeds of Drāviḍians and aborigines. Hence Hindūism is something very different from Brāhmanism, though the one is derived from the other. Hindūism is like a huge irregular structure which has spread itself over an immense surface by continual additions and accretions. Its present aspect is that of an ancient overgrown fabric, with no apparent unity of design—patched, pieced, restored and enlarged in all directions, inlaid with eveiy variety of idea, and, although looking as if ready at any moment to fall into ruins, still extending itself so as to cover every hole and corner of available ground, and still held together, and kept in its place, because supported by a hard foundation of Brāhmanism and caste. It is only, however, by the practice of a kind of universal toleration and receptivity—carried on through more than two thousand years—that Hindūism has arrived at its present condition.[1] It has first borne with and then accepted, and so to speak, digested and assimilated something from all creeds. It has opened its doors to all comers on the two conditions of admitting the spiritual supremacy of the Brāhmans; and conforming to certain caste-rules about food, intermarriage, and professional pursuits. In this manner it has adopted much of the Fetishism of the Negrito aborigines of India; it has stooped to the practices of various hill tribes, and has not scrupled to encourage the adoration of the fish, the boar, the serpent, rocks, stones, and trees; it has borrowed ideas from the various cults of the Drāviḍian races, and it may even owe something to Christianity. Above all, it has appropriated, as we have seen, nearly every doctrine

---

[1] Moor, in his 'Pantheon' (p. 402), tells us that a learned Paṇḍit once observed to him that the English were a new people, and had only the record of one Avatāra, but the Hindūs were an ancient people, and had accounts of a great many, and that if the Purāṇas were examined, they would probably be found to record the incarnation of Christ.

of Buddhism except its atheism, its denial of the eternity of soul, and its levelling of caste-distinctions.

Of course it will be held that in investigating the causes of the development of Hindūism, and its capacity for almost universal adaptation, we are bound in fairness to examine it from the standpoint of the Hindūs themselves; we ought to go to the Hindū's own authorities; we must appeal to the Veda, the Upanishads and the philosophical works founded on them.

What then have we already learnt about the creeds inculcated by these books? We know that they teach pantheism pure and simple. But they do more, they propound a most subtle theory of evolution and development.

Their doctrine is, that the one sole, self-existing Supreme Self, the only really existing Essence, the one eternal Germ of all things, delights in infinite expansion, in infinite manifestations of itself, in infinite creation, dissolution, and re-creation, through infinite varieties and diversities of operation.

This is, so to speak, the preamble of Hindūism, and it is stated with great poetical power in a celebrated hymn of the Ṛig-veda, part of which has been transtated at page 26.

The very name 'Brahman' (neut. from root *bṛih*, 'to grow') given to the Eternal Essence, is expressive of this *growth*, this *expansion*, this universal *development* and *diffusion*.

Hence, all visible form is an emanation from God, and hence, to begin with the lowest visible objects,—stones, rivers, mountains, plants, trees, animals, and men—these are but steps in the infinite evolution of his being. Hence, also a series of higher forms of existence, such as demigods, good and evil spirits, inferior gods, superior gods, is traceable upwards in an ascending scale from man, till three principal divine personages, each associated with a consort, to show that male and female, man and wife, are ever indissolubly united as the sources of reproduction—are reached. These three gods are the first and highest manifestations of the Eternal Essence, and are typified by the three letters composing the mystic syllable *OM* or *AUM*. They constitute the well-known *Tri-mūrti* or Triad of divine forms which characterizes Hindūism.

It is usual to describe these three gods as Creator, Preserver, and Destroyer, but this gives a very inadequate idea of their complex characters. Nor does the conception of their relationship to each other become clearer when it is ascertained that their functions are constantly interchangeable, and that each may take the place of the other, according to the sentiment expressed by the greatest of Indian poets, Kālidāsa (Kumāra-sambhava, Griffith, vii. 44):—

> In those three Persons the one God was shown—
> Each first in place, each last—not one alone;
> Of S'iva, Vishṇu, Brahmā, each may be
> First, second, third among the blessed Three.[1]

Nor does the doctrine of *Tri-mūrti* derive much

---

[1] There is a well-known Tri-mūrti sculptured out of the rock in the caves of Elephanta, at Bombay. Three majestic heads are represented springing out of one body. The triangle (*Tri-koṇa*) is used by the Hindūs to symbolize this triune coequality.

elucidation from the mystical explanation given of it by Indian philosophers, who assert that the Eternal, self-existent Spirit willed to invest himself with the three *Guṇas*, or binding qualities of matter; to wit, with that of activity (*rajas*) in order to become a male person, *Brahmā* (nom. case, masc.) the Creator,—with that of goodness (*sattva*), to become *Vishṇu*, the Pervader, Maintainer, and Preserver of the universe when created,—with that of darkness (*tamas*), to become *Rudra*, the Destroyer of the same universe when dissolved;[1] these three divine personages being themselves subject to the universal law of dissolution at the end of a Kalpa or æon of time, when they all three again become simple Soul (*Kevalātman*).

In real fact the idea of a Tri-mūrti or triple personification was developed gradually, and as it grew, received numerous accretions. It was first dimly shadowed forth and vaguely expressed in the Ṛig-veda, where, as we have seen a triad of principal gods, Agni, Indra, and Sūrya (see p. 24), is recognized, Indra being often identified or associated with Vāyu, and with Rudra, and with the Maruts or storm-gods.

Besides these, a god Vishṇu is sometimes named in the Veda, as a manifestation of the solar energy; and the point which distinguishes him from the others is his striding over the seven worlds in three paces (see p. 101).

---

[1] As Vishṇu appears to be connected with the day, sun, and light, so S'iva in some of his attributes seems to be associated with the close of day, the moon, and darkness. See the account of the three Guṇas under the description of the Sānkhya philosophy in the Appendix at the end of this volume (p. 194).

Subsequently he takes a foremost place among the twelve *Ādityas*, or distinct forms of the sun in the twelve months of the year (see p. 23). In the Brāhmaṇas he is identified with sacrifice (*Yajna*), and once described as a dwarf (Vāmana; Śatapatha-brāhmaṇa xiv. i. 1, 6, i. 2, 55).

In Manu's law-book, on the other hand, which stands at the head of Smṛiti (see p. 14), there is nothing to support the theory of a triad of presiding deities; although Brahman, the universal Soul, is represented as unfolding his essence in the form of Brahmā, the creator of all things; and other visible manifestations of the Deity are recognized as in the Veda. Vishṇu and Hara (= Śiva) are certainly mentioned once (xii. 121), but only as present in the human body, the former imparting movement to its muscles, the latter bestowing strength.

Probably the second phase of the doctrine of triple manifestation was about contemporaneous with the progress of the Buddhistic movement. The Vedic Agni, the personification of creative heat, with a little extension of his attributes and functions, passed into the god Brahmā, the creator; while the sun-god, Vishṇu, and the storm-god, Rudra, with a slight change in their functions but without change in their names, became respectively the world-upholder and world-dissolver. At first, however, the doctrine was not sufficiently developed to satisfy the cravings of the human heart for a religion of faith and love—of faith in a personal God, and of responsive love for a God sympathizing with and loving his creatures. Nor was there sufficient to meet the demands of two other constituent parts of man's complex nature,—for a religion of worldly activity on the one hand, and of austerity and self-suppression on the other.

The idea, therefore, of Brahmā the creator was soon expanded. He was regarded in other aspects, both as a personification of all manifested matter,[1] and as the Lord and Father of all beings (*Prajāpati*). In this latter character he is represented in the Veda as having sacrificed himself for the good of his creatures (see p. 36), and it is remarkable that, although Brahmā is now only worshipped in one principal place[2] in India (Pushkara, near Ājmīr), yet many places are held sacred because supposed to be consecrated by sacrifices performed by him after the act of creation.

But this was not all. He was made to possess a double nature, or, in other words, two characters—one quiescent, the other active. The active was called his Śakti, and was personified as his wife, or the female half of his essence. The Śakti of the creator ought properly to represent the female creative capacity, but the idea of the blending of the male and female principles in creation seems to have been transferred to Śiva and his Śakti Pārvatī. Brahmā with his four faces was then connected with the utterance of the four Vedas, and the worship which was his due was transferred to the Brāhmans, regarded as his peculiar offspring and, as it were, his mouth-pieces;

---

[1] To denote the gravity of matter, the Vāhana, or vehicle on which the god Brahmā is supposed to ride, is a Hansa or goose.

[2] I was told, when travelling in India, that there is one other place (Idur) where homage is paid to Brahmā.

while his consort Sarasvatī, once a river-goddess, was regarded as the goddess of speech and learning, and inventress of the Sanskṛit language and letters.[1]

Again, the idea of a separate divine person—Vishṇu—whose functions were those of pervading, upholding, and preserving, was also soon expanded, and easily spread into numerous ramifications. It was from this idea that the doctrine of incarnation, to which we shall refer at greater length in the next chapter, was ultimately evolved. Moreover, a *S'akti*, or wife, called Lakshmī, goddess of good fortune, was assigned to this second person of the Triad.

Thirdly.—Inasmuch as destruction necessarily leads to re-creation and reproduction, the idea of the god Rudra was also easily extended, so that a great variety of names, attributes, and functions, properly belonging to other deities, were gathered under this third person of the Triad.[2]

---

[1] The river Sarasvatī was to the earlier Hindūs what the Ganges was to the later: she was infused with divinity, and her influence permeated the writers of the Vedic hymns; she is sometimes identified with the Vedic goddess, *Vāć*, speech, and invoked, as the patroness of science. *Sarasvatī-pūjā* is performed on the *S'rī-panćamī*, the name of a festival kept on the fifth of the light half of Māgha, on which day books and writing implements are held sacred, and not used (see p. 182).

[2] He has certainly a few more names than Vishṇu, one thousand and eight being specified in the 69th chapter of the S'iva-purāṇa, and in the 17th chapter of the Anuśāsana-parvan of the Mahā-bhārata. The latter book, however, also gives a thousand names of Vishṇu. Of course many of the names of S'iva are merely epithets descriptive of his attributes; *e.g.*, *Viśveśvara*, 'lord of the universe'; *Tri-lоćana*, 'three-eyed'; *Nīla-kaṇṭha*, 'blue-throated,' his neck being blue, through the

He has, at least, three quite distinct characters, each of which has a female or active energizing counterpart (*S'akti*).

In the first place, as *Rudra*, or Mahākāla, he is the destroying and dissolving power of nature; when he is either a personification of all matter resolving itself into its constituent elements, or of Kāla, 'Time,' the great Dissolver[1]; the more active principle of destruction being assigned to his consort Kālī.

Then, in the second place, as *S'iva, Sadā-śiva, S'ankara, S'ambhu*—the eternally blessed one, or causer of blessings—he is the eternal reproductive power of nature, perpetually restoring and reproducing itself after dissolution, under which mysterious character he is often identified with the eternal creative essence[2] and even with the great impersonal eternal spirit, as the one great God (*Mahā-deva*) and supreme Lord (*Īśvara*)[3]. Hence in this character he is rather represented by a symbol (the *linga* and *yoni* combined[4]) than by any human personification; and

stain of the poison produced at the churning of the ocean, and swallowed by him; *Kapālin*, 'wearing skulls'; *Candra-śekhara*, 'moon-crested'; *Girīśa*, 'lord of the hills'; *Gangā-dhara*, 'supporter of the Ganges,' which was supposed to issue from Vishṇu's foot on the matted locks of Śiva, who thus broke its fall before it descended on the Himālaya.

[1] At the caves of Ellora, which I have lately visited, his form is wonderfully carved to represent the skeleton figure of Death.

[2] Sometimes S'iva is said to manifest himself under eight forms—ether, air, fire, water, earth, the sun, the moon, and the sacrificing priest.

[3] When the word Īśvara occurs at the end of a compound, it generally denotes S'iva.

[4] Probably reproductive energy is denoted by his vehicle or companion the bull.

temples to hold this symbol, which is of a double form to express the blending of the male and female principles in creation, are probably the most numerous of any temples now to be seen in India. There can be no doubt, in fact, that the supreme creative power is still universally worshipped throughout India, under the name of Śiva, and his Śakti, *Jagan-mātṛi*, mother of the world, instead of Brahmā and Sarasvatī; if, indeed, it be not probable that the first person of the Triad is really the great god, whose functions are implied by the *linga* and *yoni*, though his name has been changed and his office and character mixed up with those of the third person.

Then, in the third place, this third member of the Tri-mūrti is the great representative Yogī and Tapasvī, who has attained the highest perfection in meditation and austerity, and is thence called *Mahāyogī*. In this character he appears as an austere naked ascetic (*Dig-ambara*), with body covered with ashes and matted hair (*Dhūrjaṭi*), abiding fixed and immovable (*sthāṇu*) in one spot, teaching men by his own example the power to be acquired by mortification of the body, suppression of the passions, and abstract contemplation, as leading to the loftiest spiritual knowledge, and ultimately to union with the great spirit of the universe.

This third character of the third person of the Triad seems to have been a later invention of the Brāhmans to take the place of the Buddha[1] the

[1] I noticed in more than one place, while travelling in India, that idols which were once evidently images of Buddha, now do duty as images of S'iva.

memory of whose personal example as a self-denying ascetic they sought thus to neutralize. In this character of the representative ascetic, as in that of the Reproducer, he is also sometimes called the 'Blessed one' (Śiva).

There are yet two other characters of the third person of the Triad, which seem to have been assigned to him by the Brāhmans to satisfy the religious instincts of the aboriginal tribes, and serve as substitutes for their wild demoniacal gods. In the first of these, which is a modification and adaptation derived from his first character of dissolver of the universe, he is the terrible destroyer (*Bhairava*) delighting in destruction for its own sake, though it should be noted that this malignant character is more connected with his wife Kālī, than with himself. In this character he is also called Bhūteśvara, 'lord of spirits or demons,' and is depicted as haunting cemeteries and burning-grounds wearing serpents for garlands, and a string of skulls for a necklace,[1] sometimes surrounded with troops (*gaṇa*) of imps and spirits (*bhūta*), and sometimes trampling on rebellious demons who have acquired too great power.

His fifth character is the entire reverse of ascetical. In this he is a sort of representative free-liver, a wild jovial god, fond of dancing and drink, living in the

[1] Sometimes he has a tiger's skin, and he is often associated with a tiger, as his wife Durgā is borne on that animal. Sometimes he has an elephant's skin on his shoulders, which once belonged to a demon said to have been killed by him. He is also associated with an antelope, and sometimes carries a kind of drum called ḍamaru, and a staff with a skull at the top called Khatvānga.

Himālaya mountains with his wife, often dancing with her the Tāṇḍava dance, and surrounded with dwarfish, buffoon-like troops (*gaṇa*) of attendants, who, like their master, are excited by drinking. This is the character in which he is worshipped by Tāntrikas.

And here we may observe that in every one of his characters the consort of Śiva is not only his counterpart, but generally represents an intensification of his attributes.

As destructress she is *Kālī*, as reproducer she is symbolized by the *Yoni*, or she is the type of beauty in *Umā*, or she is the mother of the universe in *Jagan-mātṛi*. She has also her forms as a female ascetic (*yoginī*), as a malignant being delighting in blood (*Bhairavī Durgā*), and as a mountaineer (*Pārvatī*).

We have thus made good our assertion that the third member of the Tri-mūrti, and his consort do, in fact, represent the gathering together, and unifying in one personality numerous attributes, properties, and functions belonging to various deities and various divine forces.

The destructive energies of the atmosphere exhibited in wind and storm, and personified in the Veda as Vāyu, Rudra, and the Maruts; the all-consuming potency of time; the fertilizing properties present in dew and rain; the almighty agencies operating in creation once personified as Brahmā; the same agencies operating in re-creation and reproduction; the power of asceticism once exhibited in the Buddha; the grace of perfect beauty supposed to be specially present in Śrī or Lakshmī; the mysterious efficacy of magic and illusion (*māyā*); the terrific agencies and operations of demons and spirits, and finally the all-pervading influence of the impersonal soul of the universe—all these have been collected and centralized in one god, whose chief name is the 'Blessed one' (*S'iva*), whose person is supposed to be half male and half female, and whose triple eye and trident probably symbolize his combining the attributes of the Triad in himself.[1]

---

[1] These may denote his triple character of Destroyer, Reproducer, and Contemplative Ascetic, as the five faces with which he is sometimes represented may denote his fivefold character. Or may these five faces be connected with the five Saṃhitas of the Veda? Some think his three eyes refer to time, present, past, and future, the crescent moon on his head also symbolizing his power over the measurement of time.

CHAPTER VIII.

DEVELOPMENT OF ŚAIVISM, VAISHṆAVISM AND THE DOCTRINE OF INCARNATION.

A WORSHIPPER of the god Śiva, as described in the last chapter is called a Śaiva, and the preference given to the worship of this god may, for convenience, be called Śaivism. On the other hand, a worshipper of Vishṇu is called a Vaishṇava, and the preference given to the adoration of any of the forms of Vishṇu may conveniently be càlled Vaishṇavism.

It is scarcely too much to say that the creeds indicated by these two terms Śaivism and Vaishṇavism (see pp. 11, 12) constitute the very life and soul of modern Hindūism. Moreover, it should be clearly understood that Śaivism and Vaishṇavism are not opposite or incompatible creeds. They represent different lines of religious thought, like the differences which prevail in Europe; such lines being quite allowable within the limits of one and the same system. Śaivas and Vaishṇavas do in fact acquiesce to a certain extent in each other's views, but each lays an exaggerated stress on particular doctrines (see pp. 11, 12); and these differences eventually led to a temporary antagonism. Even in the present day, when universal toleration is the rule, Śaivas and Vaishṇavas like to maintain their distinct characteristics, which they exhibit conspicuously to the eye by the sectarian mark on their foreheads, made with red, yellow, and white pigments; the mark of the Vaishṇavas being two perpendicular strokes meeting below in a curve, which denote the footprint of Vishṇu, while that of the Śaivas consists of three horizontal lines, made with white or grey ashes (*vibhūti*). The Vaishṇava mark is called *Ūrdhva-puṇḍra*, the Śaiva is called *Tri-puṇḍra*.

Although the worship of Śiva is prevalent everywhere throughout India, no temples being so common as those which enshrine his symbol (the *lingam*), and although all classes of the Hindūs, and especially the Śāktas, or worshippers of the female principle (*S'akti*), pay him the highest respect as husband of the goddess, variously called Kālī, Durgā, Jagad-dhātrī, Mātṛi, &c., yet those who select the male god Śiva as their chosen divinity—that is to say, the divinity in whose *mantra* they are initiated, and to whom they look for special aid in the attainment of salvation—are comparatively insignificant in number.[1] They are chiefly religious mendicants, Yogīs, Gosāins, or Gosavins, Sannyāsīs, or, as they are often improperly called, Fakīrs.

In fact, the third member of the Tri-mūrti, whether as Destroyer, or as Reproducer and Creator, or as chief of ascetics, is too impersonal and too severe a god for the multitude. He occupies too lofty a position above ordinary mortals. He is a stern divinity,

---

[1] Dr. Rājendralāḷa Mitra, in his 'Antiquities of Orissa' (p. 137-138), says that it is the office of the Guru to initiate a disciple in the secret *Mantra* of the particular god he elects for his salvation, and that there is scarcely one in a hundred Gurus whose vocation is to impart the *Mantra* of S'iva.

to be approached with awe, and propitiated with reverence and fear, rather than with faith, trust, and love. This will be clear from the description in the preceding chapter. It is also shown by the sort of worship performed at his shrines.

In all the temples of Vishṇu, Kṛishṇa, and Rāma the chief daily ceremony, after washing and dressing the idol, and burning lights and incense before it, consists in offering it food of some kind,—boiled rice, grain cooked and uncooked, sweetmeats, fruit, &c., on the essence of which the deity is supposed to feed, as if he were in need of nourishment like a human being, while the remains (called *prasāda* or *mahā-prasāda*) are consumed by his worshippers. Moreover, the idols of these gods are constantly decorated with flowers and costly ornaments, especially on festive occasions. But in the case of Śiva, who, in one of his characters, is the chief of ascetics, no food is generally offered (except, perhaps at some centres of worship, such as those of Benares and Bhuvaneśvara). The daily ceremonials are of an austerely simple kind. Water from a sacred river is poured on his symbol, with perhaps a few oblations of flowers, but often there is nothing presented by worshippers but the Vilva leaf;[1] and it is remarkable that even in cases when food is offered to this divinity it is not allowed to be eaten by his votaries, according to the Brāhmanical rule, "leaves, flowers, fruit, and

---

[1] The leaf of the Vilva or *Bel* tree is typical of S'iva's attributes, because triple in form. This plant is also said to be pervaded by the presence of his wife Durgā.

water become unfit to be consumed after being consecrated to Śiva."[1]

It is clear, therefore, that a more personal, and so to speak, human god than Śiva was needed for the mass of the people,—a god who could satisfy the yearnings of the human heart for a religion of faith (*bhakti*)—a god who could sympathize with and condescend to human wants and necessities. Such a god was found in the second member of the Tri-mūrti. It was as Vishṇu that the Supreme Being was supposed to exhibit his sympathy with human trials, and his love for the human race.

If Śiva is the great god (*Mahā-deva*) of the Hindū Pantheon to whom adoration is due from all indiscriminately, Vishṇu is certainly its most popular deity. He is the god selected by far the greater number of individuals as their saviour, protector, and friend, who rescues them from the power of evil, interests himself in their welfare, and finally admits them to his heaven (*Vaikuṇṭha*). But it is not so much Vishṇu in his own person as Vishṇu in his *incarnations*, that effects all this for his votaries.

Hindūism is like a drama in which the plot is clearly traceable, but in which the acts are numerous, and in which each succeeding act is more diversified and sensational than that which precedes. In the act which has now opened upon us, the scenes are continually shifting. We have, in fact, arrived at that phase of Hindūism when the doctrine of Tri-mūrti is almost lost sight of in the prominence given to the

---

[1] *Agrahyam S'iva-naivedyam pattram pushpam phalam jalam.*

various incarnations of the second member of the Triad.

It is probable that the primary idea of a god Vishṇu (from root *vish* or *viś*, to 'pervade'), permeating and infusing his essence into material objects, might have been connected with the personification of the infinite heavenly space, just as the idea of the god Brahmā was with that of actual manifested matter.

In the Ṛig-veda, as we have seen, Vishṇu is probably a form of the sun or penetrating solar ray, and in a well-known hymn (i. 22, 16), still commonly used by the Brāhmans;[1] he is described as striding through the seven regions of the universe[2] in three steps, and enveloping all things with the dust (of his beams).

When the doctrine of the Tri-mūrti became fully established and Vishṇu had taken his place as the second member of the Triad (see p. 91), he was often, like Śiva, identified by his worshippers with the self-existent all-pervading Spirit, and under this aspect seems to have been associated with the watery element diffusing itself everywhere before the creation of the world.

In Manu (i. 10) the Supreme Spirit is called Nārāyaṇa, as moving on the waters; in harmony with which idea Vishṇu is often represented in sculptures,

---

[1] According to Dr. Rājendralāla Mitra, it is the holiest Mantra still recited at S'rāddhas and marriage rites.

[2] There are seven lower regions, viz., *Atala*, *Vitala*, *Sutala*, *Rasātala*, *Talātala*, *Mahātala* and *Pātāla;* above which are the seven Lokas or worlds, called *Bhūr* (the earth), *Bhuvar*, *Svar*, *Mahar*, *Janar*, *Tapar*, and *Brahma*, or *Satya*. Sometimes the first three of these, the earth (Bhū), atmosphere (Bhuvar), and heavens (Svar), are supposed to comprehend all the worlds.

images, and pictures as Nārāyaṇa in human form, reposing on the thousand-headed serpent Śesha, and floating on the waters.[1]

But whether Vishṇu be connected with light, with heat, or with water, it is evident that the idea conveyed is that of a divine Pervader, infusing his essence for special functions into created things, animate and inanimate; for example, into rivers, such as the Ganges; into trees and plants, such as the Tulsī; into animals, such as a fish, a tortoise, a boar; and lastly into men.

Probably the definite shape given by the Brāhmans to the doctrine of human incarnation, was due to their perception of the fact that the success of Buddhism was in great part due to the reverence the Buddha inspired by his own personal character. He practised honestly what he preached enthusiastically. He was sincere, energetic, earnest, self-sacrificing, and devoted. Adherents gathered in thousands round the person of the consistent preacher, and the Buddha himself became the real centre of Buddhism. When he died, he ceased to exist. He became, according to his own doctrine, utterly annihilated; but the remains of his burnt body were enshrined as relics in various parts of India, and his memory was worshipped almost as earnestly as his person had been revered. The mere memory of a great man, however, cannot retain its hold on the affections of a people through many generations. The Brāhmans saw this. They knew that the religious cravings of the great mass of the

[1] A lotus, on which is seated Brahmā, the Creator, is represented as issuing from the navel of the god, while the goddess Lakshmī, Vishṇu's wife, chafes her husband's feet.

Hindūs could not long be satisfied with the worship of relics, or with homage paid to a being held to be extinct. In all probability, soon after the death of Buddha (about the 4th century B.C.), they elaborated their scheme for supplying the people with real objects of faith and adoration out of their own epic poems, the Rāmāyaṇa and Mahā-bhārata. The great Kshatriya dynasties were made to trace back their origin through Brāhmanical sages to the Sun-god and the Moon-god,[1] while the great heroes, Rāma and Kṛishṇa, were declared to be not really Kshatriyas or even human beings, but incarnations of the god Vishṇu.

And here be it noted that the idea of incarnation, like every other idea in religion, morality, and science, when manipulated by the Brāhmans, was by them subtilized, distorted, and exaggerated. Hence the incarnations (*Avatāra*) of Vishṇu which were undertaken reasonably enough for preserving the world when in pressing emergencies, especially when in danger of ruin from some undue acquisition of power on the part of evil demons, are said to be of five kinds and degrees.

1st, the full human incarnation, as that of *Kṛishṇa*; *2ndly*, the partial human incarnation, consisting of half the god's essence, as in the *Rāma* of the Rāmāyaṇa, commonly called Rāma-ćandra; *3rdly*, the quarter incarnation, as in Rāma's brother *Bharata*,

[1] As Vishṇu is connected with Sūrya, the Sun, so S'iva is connected with Soma, the Moon, who is a male deity in Hindū mythology. One name for the god S'iva is moon-crested (see pp. 92, 96).

4thly, the incarnation consisting of an eighth of the god's essence, as in Rāma's two other brothers, Lakshmaṇa and Śatrughna; and *5thly*, the infusion of divine virtues or qualities into ordinary men, animals, and inanimate objects.[1]

Vishṇu's ten principal incarnations[2] may be briefly described as follows:

1. *Matsya*, 'the fish.' In this, Vishṇu became a fish to save Manu, the progenitor of the human race, from the universal deluge. This Manu was not the grandson of Brahmā and reputed author of the law-book, but the seventh Manu, or Manu of the present period, called Vaivasvata. He is represented as conciliating the favour of the Supreme Being by his austerities in an age of universal depravity. Hence, like Noah, he was miraculously warned of the coming deluge, and was commanded to build a ship and go on board with the seven Ṛishis, or patriarchs, and the seeds of all existing things. The flood came, Manu went on board, and Vishṇu took the form of a fish with a horn on its head, to which the ship was fastened by a cable. The ship was then drawn along by the fish and secured to a high crag till the flood had passed.

Another account of this incarnation makes Vishṇu, after rescuing Manu, destroy a demon named Hayagrīva, who, while Brahmā was asleep at the end of a Kalpa, stole the Vedas, and

---

[1] Often in modern times, men whose lives have been made remarkable by any peculiar circumstances, have been canonized after death, and held to be partial incarnations of the deity. Again, not only are many animals and different kinds of stones held to be permeated by the divine presence at all times, but there were special occasions on which Vishṇu took the form of animals to rescue the world in great emergencies, as in the first three Avatāras enumerated above.

[2] The Bhāgavata-purāṇa gives twenty-two incarnations of Vishṇu.

thereby caused mankind to fall into the depths of ignorance and impiety.

A third account in the Vana-parvan of the Mahābhārata (line 12,746), makes the fish an incarnation of the god Brahmā.

2. *Kūrma*, 'the tortoise.' In this he descended to aid in recovering and producing certain valuable articles, some of which were supposed to have been lost during the deluge. For this purpose he stationed himself as a tortoise at the bottom of the sea of milk,[1] that his back might serve as a pivot for the mountain Mandara, around which the gods and demons twisted the great serpent Vāsuki. They then stood opposite to each other, and using the snake as a rope and the mountain as a churning-stick, churned the ocean of milk for the production of fourteen precious and typical things. 1. The *Amṛita*, or nectar conferring immortality. 2. *Dhanvantari*, the physician of the gods, holder of the cup of *Amṛita*. 3. *Lakshmī* or *S'rī*, goddess of good fortune and beauty. 4. *Surā*, goddess of wine. 5. *Candra*, the moon. 6. *Rambhā*, a nymph, prototype of a lovely, amiable woman. 7. *Uććaiḥ-śravas*, a wonderful horse, prototype of the race of horses. 8. *Kaustubha*, a wonderful jewel. 9. *Pārijāta*, a tree yielding all desires. 10. *Surabhi*, the cow of plenty. 11. *Airāvata*, a wonderful elephant, prototype of the elephant race. 12. *S'ankha*, a shell, supposed, when blown as a horn, to insure victory. 13. *Dhanus*, an unerring bow. 14. *Visha*, poison.

3. *Varāha*, 'the boar.' In this form (symbolical of strength), Vishṇu descended to deliver the world from the power of a demon called Hiraṇyāksha, who had seized the earth and carried it down into the lowest depths of the sea. Vishṇu, as a boar, dived into the abyss, and after a contest of a thousand years, slew the monster and raised the earth. In earlier legends the universe is represented as a mass of water, and the earth, being submerged, was upheaved by the tusks of the divine boar.

---

[1] This is one of the seven concentric circular seas surrounding the seven concentric circular continents of the earth (see 'Indian Wisdom,' p. 419).

It is remarkable that the first three incarnations are all connected with the tradition of a universal deluge.

4. *Nara-sinha*, 'the man-lion.' In this, Vishṇu assumed the shape of a creature, half man, half lion, to deliver the world from the tyranny of a demon called Hiranya-kaśipu, who had obtained a boon from Brahmā that he should not be slain by either god or man or animal. Hence he became so powerful that he usurped the dominion of the three worlds, and appropriated the sacrifices made to the gods. When his pious son Prahlāda praised Vishṇu, the demon tried to destroy the boy, but Vishṇu appeared out of a pillar in the form Nara-sinha and tore Hiraṇya-kaśipu to pieces.

These four first incarnations are said to have taken place in the Satya or first age of the four ages of the world.

5. *Vāmana*, 'the dwarf.' In the second or Tretā age, Vishṇu descended as a dwarf to deprive the demon Bali (who resembles Rāvaṇa and Kansa in the stories of Rāma and Kṛishṇa) of the dominion of the three worlds. Vishṇu presented himself before him as a diminutive man, and solicited as much land as he could step in three paces. When his request was granted, he strode in two steps over heaven and earth, but out of compassion left the lower world, Pātāla (see p. 101, note 2) in the demon's possession.

6. *Paraśu-rāma*, 'Rāma with the axe.' In this, Vishṇu was born, as the son of the Brāhman Jamad-agni and descendant of Bhṛigu, in the second age, to prevent the Kshatriyas from arrogating dominion over the Brāhmanical caste. Paraśu-rāma is said to have cleared the earth twenty-one times of the whole Kshatriya class.

7. *Rāma* (commonly called Rāma-ćandra, 'the mild or moon-like Rāma'), the hero of the Rāmāyaṇa, son of King Daśaratha of the Solar race, and therefore a Kshatriya. Vishṇu took this form at the close of the second or Tretā age, to destroy the demon Rāvaṇa (see p. 110).

8. *Kṛishṇa*, 'the dark god,' the most popular of all the later deities of India. This incarnation of Vishṇu at the end of the Dvāpara or third age of the world, as the eighth son of Vasudeva and Devakī, of the Lunar race, was for the destruction of

the tyrant Kansa, the representative of the principle of evil, corresponding to Rāvaṇa in the previous incarnation.

The details of the later life of Kṛishṇa have been interwoven with the later portions of the Mahā-bhārata, but they do not belong to the plot, and they might be omitted without impairing its unity. He is certainly not the hero of the great epic. He appears as a great chief who takes the part of the real heroes—the Pāṇḍavas—and his claims to deification are often disputed. His earlier days and juvenile feats, though not found in the oldest parts of the Mahā-bhārata, may be gathered from the Hari-vanśa and Purāṇas, especially the tenth book of the Bhāgavata-purāṇa, from which we learn as follows :—

Vasu-deva (a descendant of the Yadu who, with Puru, as sons of Yayāti, formed the two branches of the Lunar dynasty) had two wives, Rohiṇī and Devakī. The latter had eight sons, of whom the eighth was Kṛishṇa. It was predicted that one of these would kill Kansa, king of Mathurā, and cousin of Devakī. He therefore imprisoned Vasu-deva and his wife, and slew their first six children. The seventh, Bala-rāma, was abstracted from Devakī's womb, transferred to that of Rohiṇī, and thus saved. The eighth was Kṛishṇa, born with black skin, and the mark called *S'rī vatsa* on his breast.[1] His father, Vasu-deva, escaped from Mathurā with the child, and, favoured by the gods, found a certain herdsman named Nanda, whose wife, Yaśodā, had just given birth to a daughter whom Vasudeva conveyed to Devakī, after substituting his own son in its place. Nanda took the infant Kṛishṇa and settled first in Gokula or Vraja, and afterwards in Vṛindāvana, where Kṛishṇa and Bala-rāma grew up together, roaming in the woods, and joining in the sports of the herdsman's sons. While still a boy, Kṛishṇa destroyed the serpent Kāliya, and lifted up the mountain Govardhana on his finger to shelter the Gopīs from the wrath of Indra, who, enraged because Kṛishṇa had instigated them to the worship of Govardhana, tried to destroy them by a deluge. He is described as sporting constantly with these Gopīs, the wives

[1] The date of his birth is kept as a great festival by the Hindūs, and called *Janmāshṭamī* (see the chapter on the festivals, p. 183).

and daughters of the cowherds, of whom eight were his favourites, especially Rādhā. Kṛishṇa built Dvārakā in Gujarāt, and thither transported the inhabitants of Mathurā after killing Kansa.

According to some, Kṛishṇa is not an incarnation of Vishṇu, but Vishṇu himself; in which case Bala-rāma, 'the strong Rāma,' born at the end of the Dvāpara or third age of the world, as son of Vasu-deva and Devakī, and elder brother of Kṛishṇa, is sometimes substituted for Kṛishṇa, as the eighth incarnation of Vishṇu.

9. *Buddha.* The adoption of Buddha as an incarnation of Vishṇu was really owing to the desire of the Brāhmans to effect a compromise with Buddhism (see p. 82). The reason some give for this incarnation is that Vishṇu assumed the form of the great sceptical philosopher, in the fourth age of the world, that he might delude Daityas, demons, and wicked men, and lead them to bring destruction on themselves by despising the Veda, and neglecting caste-duties and denying the existence of the gods. But the simple fact was that the Brāhmans adopted Buddha as some of them are now adopting Christ, and making Him out to be an incarnation of Vishṇu.

10. *Kalki* or *Kalkin*, who is yet to appear at the close of the fourth or Kali age (when the world has become wholly depraved) for the final destruction of the wicked, for the re-establishment of righteousness upon the earth, the renovation of all creation, and the restoration of a new age of purity (*satya-yuga*). According to some, he will be revealed in the sky, seated on a white horse, with a drawn sword blazing like a comet. From the fact of the horse playing an important rôle in this incarnation, it is sometimes called *Aśvāvatāra.* Some of the degraded classes of India comfort themselves in their present abject condition by looking to Kalki as their future deliverer and the restorer of their social position.

Before concluding the subject of incarnation, we may observe that Vishṇu is the only member of the Tri-mūrti who can be said to have infused his essence into actual flesh and blood for the salvation of the world in times of peril and calamity. Sometimes there are allusions in the epic poems and Purāṇas to Avatāras of Brahmā and Śiva, but these are generally not so much incarnations undergone for the love of human beings, as various forms or manifestations of one or the other of these deities, especially of Śiva.

For example, there is a form of Śiva (sometimes described as his incarnation, sometimes as his son) called Vīrabhadra. He is said to have been created from Śiva's mouth, to take vengeance on the sage Daksha, who had omitted to invite Śiva and his wife to a great sacrifice, at which all the other gods were present. He is depicted as fierce and terrific, with a thousand heads, eyes, feet, and clubs. There are also eight Bhairavas, all terrific forms of Śiva, and sometimes called his incarnations. Again, there are eleven Rudras, regarded as manifestations of his destroying nature, and certain beings called Vaṭukas, which are his youthful or child-manifestations. Finally, in his female counterpart Durgā, he is supposed to have assumed an innumerable variety of different forms for the destruction of demons, and the support of the world. These, however, more properly belong to another phase of Hindūism described in the next chapter.

Since the two great epic poems, the Rāmāyaṇa and the Mahā-bhārata, were the sources whence the doctrine of incarnation was first evolved by the Brāhmans, and since the latter is especially important as furnishing the greater part of the matter of the subsequent Purāṇas, it will be well to conclude this chapter with a brief summary of their contents.

The approximate pre-Brāhmanical and pre-Buddhistic versions of the two poems may be fixed at about 500 B.C., and their first orderly completion in their Brāhmanized form may possibly have taken place in the case of the Rāmāyaṇa, about the end of the 4th or beginning of the 3rd century B.C., and in the case of the Mahā-bhārata still later.

The Rāmāyaṇa (that is *Rāma-ayana*, the goings of Rāma, the 7th incarnation of Vishṇu for the destruction of the demon Rāvaṇa), held most sacred, and equally revered by Vaishṇavas and Śaivas, is believed to be a poem (*kāvya*), by a human yet inspired author, Vālmīki. It consists of about twenty-four thousand stanzas, arranged in seven books, which narrate the story of Rāma-ćandra, whose name is a household word throughout all India, as follow:—

The first of these (called *Bāla-kāṇḍa*) describes the boyhood of Rāma. Daśaratha, king of Ayodhyā, of the Solar dynasty, had no son, a serious calamity in India. A horse-sacrifice, therefore, was performed to propitiate the gods. Four sons were then born from the three wives of Daśaratha; the eldest, Rāma, possessing half the nature of Vishṇu, from Kauśalyā; the second, Bharata, possessing a fourth part, from Kaikeyī; and the other two, Lakshmaṇa and S'atru-ghna, sharing the remaining quarter between them, from Sumitrā. While yet a stripling, Rāma was taken to the court of Janaka, king of Mithilā or Videha. He had a wonderful bow, and had given out, that the man who could bend it should win his beautiful daughter Sītā. Rāma bent the bow, and Sītā thus became his wife; and she remained his one wife—the type of wife-like devotion. The second (called *Ayodhyā-kāṇḍa*) describes the transactions in Ayodhyā and the banishment of Rāma by his father, king Daśaratha, through the jealousy of Kaikeyī, who wished her own son to become the heir-apparent. The third (called *Araṇya-kāṇḍa*) narrates the events in the forest abode of

Rāma after his banishment, including the carrying off of Sītā by the demon Rāvaṇa, king of Ceylon. The fourth (called *Kishkindhyā-kāṇḍa*) details the occurrences at Kishkindhyā, the capital city of Sugrīva, the monkey-king who was Rāma's ally in his expedition against Ceylon for the recovery of Sītā. The fifth (called *Sundara-kāṇḍa*, 'the beautiful section') gives an account of the miracles by which the passage of the straits and the arrival of the invading armies in Lankā (Ceylon) were effected. The sixth (called *Yuddha-kāṇḍa*) describes the actual war with Rāvaṇa in Lankā, the victory over his armies and his destruction by Rāma, the recovery of Sītā, the return to Ayodhyā, the reunion of the four brothers, and final coronation of Rāma. The seventh (called *Uttara-kāṇḍa*) recounts the concluding events of the history of Rāma after his coronation on returning to Ayodhyā—his sensitiveness to the gossip and scandal of the citizens, his consequent banishment of Sītā to the hermitage of Vālmīki, notwithstanding the absolute certainty of her blameless conduct during her captivity in Rāvaṇa's palace; the birth of his twin sons, Kusa and Lava, in the hermitage; his final reunion with her and translation to heaven. All this supplement to the story has been dramatized by Bhava-bhūti in his Uttara-rāma-ćaritra, and the whole previous history in his Mahā-vīra-ćaritra.

Let us now pass to the Mahā-bhārata, probably by far the longest epic poem that the world has ever produced. It is called an *Itihāsa* or 'sacred history,' but is really a collection of Itihāsas—a vast cyclopædia or thesaurus of Hindū traditions, legendary history, ethics, and philosophy, which afterwards became the source of many of the Purāṇas. It seems to have passed through several stages of construction and reconstruction, until finally arranged and reduced to orderly written shape by a Brāhman or Brāhmans, whose names have been purposely concealed, because the work is held to be too sacred to have been composed by any human author, and is therefore attributed to the divine sage Vyāsa.

The entire work consists of about 220,000 lines, in eighteen Parvans or sections, as follow:

The 1st, called *Ādi-parvan*, describes how the two brothers, Dhṛita-rāshṭra and Pāṇḍu, of the Lunar dynasty, are brought up by their uncle Bhīshma, who conducted the government of the kingdom of Hastināpura near Delhi, and how Dhṛita-rāshṭra, who is blind, has one hundred bad sons—commonly called the Kuru princes—by his wife Gāndhārī; and how the two wives of Pāṇḍu—Pṛithā (or Kuntī) and Mādrī—have five good sons, called the Pāṇḍavas or Pāṇḍu princes. The eldest, Yudhi-shṭhira, is the Hindū ideal of excellence—a pattern of justice and integrity. Bhīma, the second, is a type of brute courage and strength. Arjuna, the third, rises more to the European standard of perfection. He may be regarded as the real hero of the Mahābhārata, of undaunted bravery, yet generous and tender-hearted. Nakula and Sahadeva, the fourth and fifth, who are twins, are both amiable, noble-minded, and spirited. The eldest of Dhṛita-rashṭra's sons, called Dur-yodhana, is the type of everything evil.

II. *Sabhā-parvan*, describes the great *Sabhā* or 'assembly of princes' at Hastinā-pura, when Yudhi-shṭhira, the eldest of the five Pāṇḍavas is persuaded to play at dice with S'akuni, and loses his title to the kingdom. The five Pāṇḍavas and Draupadī, their wife, are required to live for twelve years in the woods.

III. *Vana-parvan*, narrates the life of the Pāṇḍavas in the Kāmyaka forest. This is one of the longest books, and full of episodes, such as the story of Nala and that of the Kirātārjunīya.

IV. *Virāṭa-parvan*, describes the thirteenth year of exile, and the adventures of the Pāṇḍavas who lived for that year disguised in the service of King Virāṭa.

V. *Udyoga-parvan*, recounts the preparations for war on the side of both Pāṇḍavas and Kauravas, the former being determined to recover their kingdom. Kṛishṇa and Bala-rāma, who were relations of the contending parties, resolve not to fight, but Kṛishṇa consented to act as Arjuna's charioteer.

VI. *Bhīshma-parvan*, describes how both armies join battle on Kuru-kshetra, a plain north-west of Delhi. The Kauravas are commanded by Bhīshma, who falls transfixed with arrows by Arjuna, but lingers for some time.

VII. *Droṇa-parvan*, describes how the Kuru forces are commanded by Droṇa, and how numerous battles take place. Droṇa falls in a fight with Dhṛishṭa-dyumna (son of Drupada).

VIII. *Karṇa-parvan*, tells how the Kurus are led by Karṇa; how other battles occur, in which Arjuna kills Karṇa.

IX. *S'alya-parvan*, relates how S'alya is made general of the Kuru army, and how numerous concluding battles take place, and only three of the Kuru warriors, with Duryodhana, are left alive. Bhīma and Duryodhana then fight with clubs, and Duryodhana—the chief and eldest of the Kurus—is struck down.

X. *Sauptika-parvan*, describes how the three surviving Kurus make a night attack on the camp of the Paṇḍavas, and kill all their army, but not the five Paṇḍavas.

XI. *Strī-parvan*, describes the lamentations of Queen Gāndhārī and the other wives and women over the bodies of the slain heroes.

XII. *S'ānti-parvan*, recounts the coronation of Yudhi-shṭhira in Hastinā-pura. To calm his spirit, troubled with the slaughter of his kindred, Bhīshma, still alive, instructs him at great length in the duties of kings, and gives rules for adversity and rules for attaining final emancipation.

XIII. *Anuśāsana-parvan*, continues Bhīshma's discourse. Precepts and wise advice on all subjects are given; such as the duties of kings, liberality, fasting, eating, &c., mixed up with tales, moral and religious discourses, and metaphysical disquisitions. At the conclusion of his long sermon Bhīshma dies.

XIV. *Āśvamedhika-parvan*, tells how Yudhi-shṭhira, having assumed the government, performed an Aśva-medha, or 'horse-sacrifice,' in token of his supremacy.

XV. *Āśramavāsika-parvan*, narrates how the old blind king, Dhṛita-rāshṭra, with his queen Gāndhārī, and with Kuntī, mother of the Pāṇḍavas, retires to a hermitage in the woods. After two years a forest conflagration takes place, and they immolate themselves in the fire to secure heaven and felicity.

XVI. *Mausala-parvan*, narrates the death of Kṛishṇa and Balarāma, their return to heaven, the submergence of Kṛishṇa's city, Dvārakā, by the sea, and the self-slaughter in a fight with clubs (*musala*) of Kṛishṇa's family, the Yādavas, through the curse of some Brāhmans.

XVII. *Mahāprasthānika-parvan*, describes the renunciation of their kingdom by Yudhi-shṭhira and his four brothers, and their departure towards Indra's heaven in Mount Meru.

XVIII. *Svargārohaṇika-parvan*, narrates the ascent and admission to heaven of the five Paṇḍavas, their wife Draupadī, and kindred.

The supplement, or *Harivanśa-parvan*, a later addition, recounts the genealogy and birth of Kṛishṇa and the details of his early life.

CHAPTER IX.

THE DOCTRINE OF FAITH (*bhakti*) AS DEVELOPED IN THE PURĀNAS AND TANTRAS.

THE period of the Epic poems was not marked by much rivalry between the worshippers of the three members of the Tri-mūrti. Brahmā, Vishṇu, and Śiva were at first regarded as different names for the one universal eternal essence, manifesting itself variously. Their attributes and functions were constantly interchanged without any necessary antagonism. After a time the doctrine of incarnation received definite shape, and the heroes of the Epic poems were deified as incarnations of Vishṇu. It was not, however, till a comparatively recent period that strifes and jealousies arose between the followers of Vishṇu and Śiva, and of their incarnations and manifestations, each god being identified with the Supreme Being by his worshippers. The Purāṇas were then written for the express purpose, as we have seen, of exalting one deity or the other to the highest position, while other books, called Tantras, were composed to give prominence to the worship of the female counterpart of Śiva. Moreover, the doctrine of *bhakti*, or 'salvation by faith,' which existed to a certain extent from the earliest times, and which was fully propounded in the Bhagavad-gītā, a philosophical episode of the Mahā-bhārata, (see the Appendix p. 206, for a full description of this celebrated episode), and reduced to a system by a writer called Śāṇḍilya in his Bhakti-sūtras,—became in the Purāṇas and Tantras exaggerated and perverted. The most complete devotion to the personal deities, Kṛishṇa and Rāma was enjoined by the Vaishṇavas, while the Śāktas claimed the same for Durgā. Furthermore, an absolute belief in the most extravagant miracles, alleged to have been worked by these deities, and an unreasoning acceptance of every monstrous detail of their legendary history, were insisted on; while the relationship of the human soul to the divine was described in the language of human love, and illustrated with images and allegories, suggestive of conjugal union, and even of sexual and adulterous passion.

The Purāṇas and Tantras are the true exponents of these two last and most corrupt phases of popular Hindūism, on which account both sets of books are sometimes called a fifth Veda especially designed for the masses of the people and for women.

In order to invest the former with a sacred character, a fictitious antiquity was given to them by naming them Purāṇa, 'ancient tradition,' and assigning their compilation to the ancient sage Vyāsa, the supposed arranger of the Vedas and Mahā-bhārata, and founder of the Vedānta philosophy. The work called Vāyu-purāṇa is perhaps one of the oldest of this class of writings; but an earlier date can scarcely be assigned to it than the 6th century of our era.

The Purāṇas, then, must be carefully distinguished from the Itihāsas (see p. 111). It is true that the latter furnish the raw material for the composition of the Purāṇas, but, notwithstanding this relationship, the two classes of works are very different. The Itihāsas are the legendary histories of heroic men before they were actually deified, whereas the Purāṇas are properly the history of the same heroes converted into positive gods, and made to occupy the highest position in the Hindū Pantheon.

Strictly, every Purāṇa is supposed to treat of five topics: 1. The creation of the universe; 2. Its destruction and re-creation; 3. The genealogy of gods and patriarchs; 4. The reigns and periods of the Manus; 5. The history of the Solar and Lunar races of kings. And on this account the oldest native lexicographer gives *Pańca-lakshaṇa*, 'characterized by five subjects,' as a synonym of Purāṇa. The fact that very few of the Purāṇas now extant answer to this title, and that the abstract given in the Matsya-purāṇa of the contents of all the others does not always agree with the extant works, either in the subjects described, or in number of verses enumerated, proves that, like the Rāmāyaṇa and Mahā-bhārata, they were preceded by more ancient works. In the Bhāgavata-purāṇa, six original collections are specially declared to have been taught by Vyāsa to six sages, his pupils, and these six collections may have formed the bases of the present works; those which relate to Brahmā being sometimes called *Rājasa* Purāṇas (from his own peculiar Guṇa *rajas*, see p. 88); those which exalt Vishṇu being designated *Sāttvika* (from his Guṇa *sattva*); and those which prefer Śiva being styled *Tāmasa* (from his Guṇa *tamas*).

The following are the names of the eighteen Purāṇas according to the above three divisions:—

I. The Rājasa Purāṇas, or those which relate to Brahmā, are: 1. *Brahma*, 2. *Brahmāṇḍa*, 3. *Brahma-vaivarta*, 4. *Mārkaṇḍeya*, 5. *Bhavishya*, 6. *Vāmana*.

II. The Sāttvika Purāṇas, or those which relate to Vishṇu, are: 1. *Vishṇu*, 2. *Bhāgavata*, 3. *Nāradīya*, 4. *Garuḍa*, 5. *Padma*, 6. *Vārāha*. These six are usually called Vaishṇava Purāṇas.

III. The Tāmasa, or those which glorify S'iva, are: 1. *S'iva*, 2. *Linga*, 3. *Skanda*, 4. *Agni*, 5. *Matsya*, 6. *Kūrma*. These six are usually styled S'aiva Purāṇas. For the 'Agni,' the ancient Purāṇa called '*Vāyu*' is often substituted.

Although it is certainly convenient to group the eighteen Purāṇas in these three divisions, in accordance with the theory of the Tri-mūrti or triple manifestation, it must not be supposed that the six so-called Rājasa Purāṇas are devoted to the exclusive exaltation of Brahmā, or the Tāmasa to that of Śiva. The real god of the Purāṇas may be said to be Vishṇu, since all the Purāṇas are more or less concerned with his various forms and incarnations. Moreover, underlying the teaching of all of them may be discerned the one grand pantheistic doctrine, generally found at the root of Hindū theology—whether Vedic or Purānic—the doctrine expressed in the formula *ekam eva advitīyam* (see p. 11).

Furthermore, interwoven with the radically pantheistic and Vedāntic texture of these compositions, tinged as it is with other philosophical ideas (especially the Sānkhyan doctrine of Prakṛiti), and diversified as it is with endless fanciful mythologies, theogonies, cosmogonies, and mythical genealogies, we have a whole body of erroneous teaching on nearly every subject of knowledge.

Of all the eighteen Purāṇas, the Mārkaṇḍeya is the least sectarian, while the Bhāgavata is by far the most celebrated. Perhaps the next best known is the Vishṇu.

Of the Mārkaṇḍeya, which is one of the oldest—probably as old as the 8th century of our era, part is in praise of Brahmā, and part of Vishṇu. A section of this Purāṇa, called the Devī-māhātmya or C'aṇḍī-māhātmya, is repeated at the great autumnal festival in honour of Durgā (see p. 183). It is devoted to the praise of Durgā, the chief Devī or goddess (standing alone without a husband), and of her victory over the demons, especially the buffalo demon Mahishāsur.

The Bhāgavata-purāṇa is in twelve sections or books.

Parikshit, king of Hastinā-pura, and grandson of Arjuna, was condemned, in consequence of a curse, to die by the bite of a snake in seven days, and therefore went to the banks of the Ganges to prepare for death. There he was visited by certain sages, among whom was Śuka, who answered his inquiry as to the best way for preparing for death by relating the Bhāgavata-purāṇa, as he received it from Vyāsa.

Its most important book is the tenth, which narrates the early life of Kṛishṇa, an abstract of which has already been given at p. 107.

The following story, freely translated and slightly amplified from the 89th chapter of this book, affords a good example of the view taken by the Bhāgavata-purāṇa (and, indeed, by most of the Purāṇas) of the comparative excellence of the three members of the Tri-mūrti :—

A dispute arose among the sages as to which of the three gods was greatest; so they applied to the great Bhṛigu, one of the ten Maharshis, or primeval patriarchs created by the first Manu, to determine the point. He undertook to put all three gods to a severe test, and went first to Brahmā; on approaching whom he purposely omitted an obeisance. Upon this the god's anger blazed terribly forth; but, restraining it, he was at length pacified. Next he repaired to the abode of S'iva, in Kailāsa, and omitted to return the god's salutation. The vindictive deity was enraged, his eyes flashed fire, and he raised his trident to destroy the sage; but the god's wife, Pārvatī, fell at his feet, and by her intercession appeased him. Lastly, he repaired to Vaikuṇṭha, the heaven of Vishṇu, whom he found asleep with his head on his consort Lakshmī's lap. To make a trial of his forbearance, he boldly gave the god a kick on his breast, which awoke him. Instead of showing anger, however, Vishṇu arose, and on seeing Bhṛigu, asked his pardon for not having greeted him on his first arrival. Next, he expressed himself highly honoured by the sage's blow (which he declared had imprinted an indelible mark of good fortune on his breast),[1] and then inquired tenderly whether his foot was hurt, and proceeded to rub it gently. 'This,' said Bhṛigu, 'is the mightiest god; he overpowers by the most potent of all weapons—gentleness and generosity.'

Of all the eighteen Purāṇas the Vishṇu-purāṇa conforms most nearly to the epithet *panča-lakshaṇa.* The great sage Parāśara is supposed to relate it to his disciple Maitreya. It is in six books, and is, of course, dedicated to the exaltation of Vishṇu, whom it

---

[1] This mark is called the S'rīvatsa. In some forms of Vishṇu or Kṛishṇa, such as that called Vīṭho-bā (worshipped at Paṇḍharpur) it is represented as a real footmark.

identifies with the Supreme Being. Here is an epitome of the six books:—

The first book treats of the creation of the universe; the peopling of the world and the descent of mankind from seven or nine patriarchs, sons of Brahmā; the destruction of the universe at the end of a Kalpa and its re-creation; and the reigns of kings during the first Manvantara. The second book describes the various worlds, heavens, hells, and planetary spheres, and gives the formation of the seven circular continents and concentric oceans. The third book describes the arrangement of the Vedas, Itihāsas, and Purāṇas by Vyāsa, and the institution and rules of caste, in which it follows and resembles Manu. The fourth book gives lists of kings and dynasties. The fifth book is devoted to the life of Kṛishṇa. The sixth and last book describes the deterioration of mankind during the four ages of the world called *Kṛita*, *Tretā*, *Dvāpara*, and *Kali*; the destruction of the world by fire and water, and its dissolution at the end of a Kalpa or Æon (comprising 4,320,000,000 years).

The above is a bare outline of the contents of the Vishṇu-purāṇa, which is encyclopedical, like the others, and is full of wild philosophical speculations and curious legends.

The following account of the Kali, or fourth age of the world—the age of universal degeneracy—is from book vi. 1:—

Hear what will happen in the Kali age.
The usages and institutes of caste,
Of order and of rank, will not prevail,
Nor yet the precepts of the triple Veda.
Religion will consist in wasting wealth;
In fasting and performing penances
At will; the man who owns most property
And lavishly distributes it, will gain

Dominion over others; noble rank
Will give no claim to lordship; self-willed women
Will seek their pleasure, and ambitious men
Fix all their hopes on riches gained by fraud.
The women will be fickle and desert
Their beggared husbands, loving them alone
Who give them money. Kings instead of guarding
Will rob their subjects, and abstract the wealth
Of merchants, under plea of raising taxes.
Then in the world's last age the rights of men
Will be confused, no property be safe,
No joy and no prosperity be lasting.

There are eighteen *Upa-purāṇas*, or 'secondary Purāṇas,' subordinate to the eighteen principal Purāṇas, of which the names only need be given, as follow:—

1. *Sanatkumāra*, 2. *Narasinha* or *Nṛisinha*, 3. *Nāradīya* or *Vṛihan-nāradīya*, 4. *Siva*, 5. *Durvāsasa*, 6. *Kapila*, 7. *Mānava*, 8. *Auśanasa*, 9. *Vāruṇa*, 10. *Kālikā*, 11. *Sāmba*, 12. *Nandi*, 13. *Saura*, 14. *Pārāśara*, 15. *Āditya*, 16. *Māheśvara*, 17. *Bhāgavata* (for Bhārgava ?), 18. *Vāśishṭha*. In another list the *Nandā*, *Siva-dharma*, *Brahmāṇḍa* and *Kāurma* are substituted for some of the above.

Let us now turn to the Tantras, and consider the system they inculcate, which for convenience may be called Tāntrism, or, from the Śāktas who follow it, Śāktism.

Although some of the Purāṇas and Upa-purāṇas, such as the Skanda, Brahma-vaivarta, and Kālikā, do in real truth teach Tāntrika doctrines by promoting the worship of Prakṛiti and Durgā, yet it is also true that the Tantras represent a phase of Hindūism generally later than that represented by the Purāṇas.

Indeed, Tāntrism, or Śāktism, is Hindūism arrived at its last and worst stage of medieval development.

As the most conspicuous god of the Purāṇas is Vishṇu with his incarnations, so the most prominent deity of the Tantras is Śiva with his manifestations, more especially in the innumerable forms of his female counterpart.[1]

We have already noted that the principal Hindū deities are supposed to possess a double nature, or two characters—one quiescent, the other active,—and that the active, called his *S'akti*, is personified as his wife, or as the female half of his essence, represented, as we shall see presently, on his left side. Be it now observed that, just as the male god Śiva gathered under his own personality the attributes and functions of all the principal gods, and became 'the great god' (*Mahā-deva*)—that is, the most lofty and severe god of the Hindū Pantheon,—so his female counterpart became 'the one great goddess' (*devī, mahā-devī*), who required more propitiation than any other goddess, and to a certain extent represented all other female manifestations of the Tri-mūrti, and absorbed all their functions.[2] For this reason even the wives of Brahmā and Vishṇu were said to be her daughters. According to the Vāyu-purāṇa, not only

[1] It must not, however, be forgotten that there are a few Vaishṇava Tantras which substitute Rādhā, the favourite wife of Kṛishṇa, for Durgā, wife of S'iva.

[2] Kullūka (Manu, ii. 1) says, *S'rutir dvividhā vaidikī tāntrikī ća*, 'revelation is twofold, Vedic and Tāntrik.' Besides the name Āgama there are two other names,—*Yāmala* and *Dāmara*—applied to certain classes of Tantras.

was Śiva himself of a twofold nature, male and female, but his female nature also became twofold, one half *Asita*, or white, and the other half *Sita*, or black, each of these again becoming manifold. The white, or mild nature, became ṣeparated into the Śaktis, called *Umā*, *Gaurī*, *Lakshmī*, *Sarasvatī*, &c.; the black, or fierce nature, into those called *Durgā*, *Kālī* *C'aṇḍī*, *C'āmuṇḍā*, &c. In short, all the other Śaktis seem to have been included by the Śāktas under the Śakti or energy of Śiva, which eventually developed into innumerable separate manifestations and personifications of all the forces of nature, physical, physiological, moral, and intellectual. These forces, or rather the deified personalities presiding over them, were grouped in separate classes, such as *Mātṛis* or *Mātṛikās*, 'divine mothers'; *Yoginīs*, 'goddesses endowed with magical powers,' &c. They are too numerous to be separately named, various classifications having been adopted for the sake of disposing the female manifestations of Śiva, like the male incarnations of Vishṇu (see p. 103), under different degrees of participation in the divine essence; such as the full (*pūrṇa-śakti*, *mūla-prakṛiti*), the partial (*anśa-rūpiṇī*), the still more partial (*kalā-rūpiṇī*), and the partial of the partial (*kalānśa-rūpiṇī*); the lowest including mortal women in various degrees, from Brāhman women downwards, who are all worshipped as forms of the divine mother upon earth.[1] There are, however, certain principal female personifications

[1] In the case of the Vaishṇava Tantras, Rādhā, wife of Kṛishṇa, represents the full manifestation, and the Gopīs the partial.

which it will be well to specify; for just as the Vaishnavas worship ten chief male incarnations of the god Vishṇu, so the Śāktas worship ten chief female manifestations of the god Śiva, or rather of his Śakti or energy. They are called Mahāvidyās, as sources of supreme knowledge, or of the knowledge which confers supreme power; and their names are as follow:—

1. *Kālī* (sometimes called S'yāmā). 2. *Tārā*, represented as a stouter figure than Kālī, with legs in a different attitude. 3. *Siddha-vidyā*. 4. *Mātangī*. 5. *Bhairavī*. 6. *Chinna-mastakā*, represented as a naked headless goddess standing upon a human couple and holding in one hand a blood-stained scimitar and in the other her own severed head, which drinks the warm blood gushing from her headless trunk. 7. *Shoḍaśī* (sometimes called Tripurā). 8. *Bhuvaneśvarī* (sometimes called Manjughosha). 9. *Dhūmavatī*. 10. *Vagalā* or Bagalā (sometimes called Bagalā-mukhī). The last four are milder incarnations.

Besides these, there are principal Mātṛis, Yoginīs, &c., too numerous to be specified.[1]

In fact, this phase of Hindūism may be described as a kind of worship of *force*, branching out into endless modifications and correlations, though why these should be regarded as female deities rather than as male is not at first sight clear.

In all probability the Tāntrika doctrine owes its

[1] Some lists give seven, some eight, nine, sixteen, fifty-two chief Mātṛis; some upwards of a hundred. The Yoginīs are sometimes represented as created by Durgā, sometimes as forms of that goddess ten millions in number. Again, according to some, there are only eight chief Yoginīs, according to others sixty-five.

development to the popularizing of the Sānkhya theory of *Purusha*, the primeval male or supreme soul of the universe, and *Prakṛiti*, the active producing principle, each distinct from the other, yet each uniting in the act of creation. In harmony with this idea the images of the 'great god' Śiva sometimes represent him (see p. 96) as *Ardha-nārī*, that is, a being consisting of two halves, the male half being on his right side, and the female on his left.

It may easily be imagined that a creed like this was likely to degenerate into impure doctrines, and that result was actually brought about; for those who applied the principle of faith (*bhakti*) to the double nature of the deities, finally resolved themselves into two classes,—the first called *Dakshiṇā-ćārins*, 'right-hand worshippers,' who make the Purāṇas their real Veda (*nigama*). These are devoted (*bhakta*) to Śiva, Vishṇu, Kṛishṇa, and their wives, but merely in their characters of gods and goddesses, not with any undue preference for the female divinity, and not with any implication of impure ideas; the second called *Vāmāćārins*, 'left-hand worshippers,' who are followers of the Kaulopanishad, and make that Upanishad and the Tantras their own peculiar Veda (*āgama*). These devote themselves to the worship of the female counterpart of the deities, to Durgā rather than Śiva, to Rādhā rather than Kṛishṇa, and to Sītā rather than Rāma; but especially to Durgā, not as Śiva's wife, but as the goddess who presides over two quite distinct operations,—the intercourse of the sexes and the acquisition of magical powers.

And here be it noted, that just as Buddhism was the expression of a natural effort to break through the restraints of caste in one direction, so Śāktism or Tāntrism was an effort in another—the one ending in asceticism, the other in licentiousness.

The rites, or rather orgies of the left-hand worshippers, presuppose the meeting of men and women of all castes in the most unrestrained manner on terms of perfect equality.[1] They are carried on in secret, and are said to require the use of some of the five Makāras; namely,—1. *Madya*, wine; 2. *Mānsa*, flesh; 3. *Matsya*, fish; 4. *Mudrā*, parched grain;[2] 5. *Maithuna*, sexual union.[3] Each of the above is again subdivided into five. But the object of these worshippers is not merely to break through the restraint of caste and give themselves up to licentious practices. They also aim at acquiring magical and mystical powers by the use, or abuse, of Mantras, and what are called Vījas, Nyāsas, and Yantras.

---

[1] The circle they form at their meetings is called *ćakra*, and the verse cited as the authority for the temporary suppression of caste at these meetings is as follows:—*Prāpte hi Bhairave ćakre sarve varṇā dvijottamāḥ Nivṛitte Bhairave ćakre sarve varṇāḥ pṛithak pṛithak.* "On entering the circle of Bhairava, all castes are on an equality with the best of the twice-born; on leaving it, they are again separated into castes."

[2] This grain is eaten like dry biscuit with the wine and spirituous liquor. The term *Mudrā* is also used in Tāntrism to denote mystical intertwinings of the fingers so as to form symbolical figures.

[3] The union of the actual man and woman in the religion of the Tāntrikas, or left-hand worshippers, takes the place of the Linga and Yoni in that of the right-hand worshippers.

With regard to the Mantras, it should be observed that a Mantra with the Tāntrikas loses its character of a divinely inspired prayer addressed to a deity (see p. 18). It is generally, indeed, a text from the Veda, but rather from the Atharva-veda collection than from the three others, and instead of a prayer or invocation, becomes a spell or charm, the very sound of which, if properly uttered and repeated according to prescribed formularies, has, in itself, a mystical power for good or evil.

As to the Vījas, these are mystical letters or syllables employed for brevity to denote the root (*mūla*), or essential part of a Mantra, the name of the deity to whom it may be addressed, or some part of the body over which that deity presides. For example :—

Am is said to denote S'iva, *U* Vishṇu, *Hrim* the sun, *Lam* the earth, *Ṅam* the mind, *Dham* both the goddess Bhuvaneśvarī and the tongue, *Nam* both the goddess Annapūrṇā and the nose, *Pam* the ear, &c.

And here, be it observed, that the proper location or application of the several letters of the alphabet to the several parts of the body, as symbols of the Śaktis or Mātṛikās who preside over those parts is called *Nyāsa*, and plays an important part in the Tāntrik worship. Sound is held to be eternal and co-existent with the deity (according to the Mīmānsā aphorism, *S'abdo yonitvād Brahma*). Hence the letters of the alphabet being the ultimate instruments by which sounds are uttered and thoughts expressed, are considered to possess supernatural attributes, and to have in themselves a mystical and mysterious efficacy. They are supposed to represent the several Mātṛikās, or Śaktis (forces), which sustain the corporeal organs, and govern the vital functions. Let a man only acquaint himself with the proper pronunciation and application both of the Mantras and of their Vījas, or radical letters, and he acquires the power of working prodigies to any extent he pleases.[1]

As to the *Yantras* these are mystical diagrams—generally combinations of triangular figures, like the inverted triangles of the Freemasons—supposed to possess occult powers. Each of the Śaktis has a Yantra assigned to her, which Yantras are sometimes placed in the centre of representations of lotuses, the Vīja of the goddess being also inscribed a certain number of times on each petal.

From the foregoing statement it will justly be inferred that the Tantras are generally mere manuals of mysticism, magic, and superstition of the worst and most silly kind.

Theoretically, however, they are very different, and, as a matter of fact, they are not all of this character. There are about sixty-four original Tantras, and a large number of other Tāntrik works, generally written in the form of a dialogue between the god Śiva and his wife. None of the actual Tantras have, as yet, been printed or translated in Europe. Prac-

[1] There are certain Brāhmans called Mantra-śāstrīs who make this their peculiar business. Hence the saying that 'all the universe is subject to the gods, the gods are subject to the Mantras, and the Mantras to the Brāhmans. Therefore, the Brāhmans are the gods of the universe.'

tically, they constitute a fifth Veda (in place of the Purāṇas), for the Śāktas, or worshippers of the female divine energy (*S'akti*) of the male gods, on which account the name *Āgama* is sometimes given to the original Tantras to distinguish them from *Nigama*, a name only applied to the Vedas and Purāṇas.

Every Tantra ought, like a Purāṇa, to treat of five subjects; namely,—1. The Creation; 2. The destruction of the world; 3. The worship of the gods; 4. The attainment of all objects, especially of eight superhuman powers (*siddhi*); 5. The four modes of union with the Supreme Spirit (see p. 51). Very few conform even partially to this rule. Most of them are mere hand-books for the use of practisers of a kind of witchcraft, which to Europeans appears so ineffably absurd that the possibility of any persons believing in it seems in itself almost incredible. Whole Tantras teach nothing but what may be called the science of employing unmeaning sounds for acquiring magical power over friends, and for destroying enemies and rivals.

Some give collections of spells suitable for making people enamoured, for destroying sight, for producing or preventing diseases, for injuring crops, for alchemy (*rasāyana*). Others explain the most effectual modes of worshipping the Śaktis, Mahāvidyās, Mātṛis, Yoginīs, Vaṭukas, or by whatever name the innumerable manifestations of Śiva and his wife may be called. Others simply describe the Yantras, Vījas, and Mudrās (intertwinings of the fingers) belonging to each manifestation, the places suited for the worship of each, the names of trees and plants sacred to each, or permeated by each, and the days of the year allotted to each. Some few touch on nearly every conceivable topic of human knowledge, and contain here and there really interesting matter.

So little is known about the composition of these mystical writings that it is not possible to decide at present as to which are the most ancient, and still less as to the date to be assigned to any of them. They are all said to be founded on the Kaulopanishad. It may, however, be taken for granted that the extant treatises are, like the extant Purāṇas, founded on older works; and if the oldest known Purāṇa is not older than the sixth or seventh century, an earlier date can scarcely be attributed to the oldest known Tantra. Perhaps the *Rudra-yāmala* is one of the most deservedly esteemed and most encyclopedic in its teaching.[1] Others are the *S'akti-sangama*, *Viśva-sāra*, *Mahā-nirvāṇa*, *Vīra*, *Kulārṇava* (or text-book of the Kaulas), *S'yāmā-rahasya*, *S'aradā-tilaka*, *Uḍḍīsa*, *Kāmākhyā*, *Vishṇu-yāmala*.

Full as the above works are of doubtful symbolism, they are not necessarily full of impure allusions, though the teaching contained in the best of them unquestionably tends towards licentiousness. When they are better known, their connection with a distorted view of the Sānkhyan philosophy, and with some of the corrupt forms of Buddhism, will probably be made clear.

There are also works called Vaishṇava Tantras, such as the *Gautamīya* and the *Sanat-kumāra*, but

---

[1] It is said to consist of 100,000 verses. A section of it, called Jāti-mālā, treating of caste, has been printed at Calcutta.

even in these Śiva is the narrator and his wife the supposed listener. Moreover their teaching, which makes Rādhā, the wife of Kṛishṇa, take the place of Durgā as the chief object of adoration, has the same tendency as that of the other Tantras, and equally leads to licentiousness.

It may be well to give some idea of what this Tāntrik teaching really is, by a specimen of the directions given for performing the rite called *Bhūta-śuddhi*, a rite the aim of which is to expel the evil spirits whose presence would interfere with the due performance of subsequent ceremonies. The directions are here abridged from a native work on the Durgā-pūjā of Bengal.[1]

Holding a scented flower, anointed with sandal, on the left temple, repeat *Om* to the Gurus, *Om* to Gaṇeśa, *Om* to Durgā. Then with *Omphat* rub the palms with flowers, and clap the hands thrice over the head, and by snapping the fingers towards ten different directions, secure immunity from the evil spirits. Next utter the Mantra *Ram*, sprinkle water all around, and imagine this water as a wall of fire. Let the priest identify himself with the animal spirit (*jīvātman*) abiding in man's breast, in the form of the tapering flame of a lamp, and conduct it by means of the Sushumnā nerve through the six spheres within the body upwards to the Divine Spirit. Then meditate on the twenty-four essences in nature; viz. the five cardinal elements, the five external organs of sense, the five organs of action, with those of self-consciousness and self-cogitation or egoism.

Conceive in the left nostril the Mantra *Yam*, declared to be the Vīja or root of wind; repeat it sixteen times while drawing air by the same nostril; then close the nose and hold the breath, and repeat the Mantra sixty-four times.

---

[1] The author's name is *Pratāpa-čandra Ghosha.*

Then meditate on Mātṛikā, and say, 'Help me, goddess of speech': *Am* to the forehead, *Am* to the mouth, *Im* to the right eye, *Im* to the left eye, *Um* to the right ear, *Um* to the left ear, *Im* to the right cheek, *Im* to the left cheek, *Em* to the upper lip, *Aim* to the lower lip, *Om* to the upper teeth, *Aum* to the lower teeth, *Tam*, *Tham*, *Dam*, *Dham*, and *Nam* to the several parts of the left leg, *Pam* to the right side, *Pham* to the left, *Bam* to the back, *Mam* to the stomach, *Yam* to the heart, *Ram* to the right shoulders, *Lam* to the neck-bone, *Vam* to the left shoulders, *Sam* from the heart to the right leg, *Ham* from the heart to the left leg, *Ksham* from the heart to the mouth.

CHAPTER X.

MEDIEVAL AND MODERN SECTS.

In the previous chapters we have endeavoured to trace briefly the progress of Hindūism, and have followed it to the last stage of its development in medieval times—to its darkest and worst phase, Śāktism or Tāntrism. It is believed that six or seven hundred years ago Śāktism was universally prevalent throughout the greater part of India, as indeed it still is in Bengal and many other extensive districts. This general degradation of religion through what is called the left-hand form of worship—or devotion to the female counterpart of Śiva—led to the springing up of various reforming sects, and to them we must now turn our attention. It is a subject which opens out an almost unbounded field on which to expatiate, and volumes might be written before exhausting it. Our limited space, however, restricts us to a brief notice of some of the chief sects; and at the very outset we are met by a difficulty as to what is meant by a Hindū sect?

The term is sometimes applied in a general way to five classes of worshippers, viz. the *Vaishṇavas*, *S'aivas*, and *S'āktas*, with the *Sauras*, Sun-worshippers, and *Gāṇapatyas*, adorers of Gaṇapati (Gaṇeśa), the lord of the troops of devils. But the greater number of

Hindūs are worshippers of Vishṇu, Śiva or their Śaktis; and although many display special preference for one or the other, many also pay homage to all these deities equally, without belonging to particular sects.

Moreover, all good Hindūs adore the sun (*Sūrya*) daily, and scarcely any religious rite is performed without homage being paid to him or Mantras being addressed to him, while only a few persons here and there are specially initiated into his Mantra, or select him for their special saviour. Again, all Hindūs worship the god Gaṇeśa, as the remover of obstacles at the commencement of every undertaking; some of his forms (such as Ḍhuṇḍhi-rājā at Benares) receiving special worship at solitary places. In fact, the systems we have styled Vaishṇavism, Śaivism, and Śāktism, with Sun-worship and Gaṇeśa-worship, constitute, so to speak, the chief staple of ordinary Hindūism.

Evidently, therefore, it must lead to confusion of thought if these five names are used to express sectarian separation from the every-day belief and practice of the bulk of the Hindū people. But we may legitimately employ the term 'sect' to designate separate societies or communities within the two leading systems of Vaishṇavism and Śaivism —separate divisions, in fact, of these systems themselves, originated by particular revivalist leaders for the enforcement of greater strictness of devotion to the Hindū gods, whose worship had degenerated through the influence of Buddhism, or for the propagation of their own peculiar ideas in morals and philosophy. Such divisions are called Sampradāyas, as representing the peculiar traditionary doctrine originated by such teachers, and handed down from generation to generation.

One most noticeable feature in the Sampradāyas founded by these reformers has been the exaggeration of the principle of faith and love (*bhakti*), so that even caste was subordinated to it; in other words, the making devotion to Kṛishṇa (Vishṇu) or Śiva, but especially an enthusiastic love for the former, a bond of union stronger than all social distinctions.

Those who made every other duty give way to this religious passion called themselves, not Vaishṇavas or Śaivas, but Bhāktas. They made songs, music, dancing, and waving of lights (*ārti*), take the place of the old Vedic Mantras, substituted vernacular prayers for those in Sanskṛit, and paid special adoration to the images of Kṛishṇa. Moreover, they believed that for the attainment of beatitude it was necessary to pass through five stages: 1. That of *S'ānti*, or calm contemplation of the deity; 2. That of *Dāsya*, or servitude; 3. That of *Sakhya*, or friendship; 4. That of *Vātsalya*, or filial affection; and 5. That of *Mādhurya*, or tender love.

In the practice of this *Bhakti* they knew no distinction of caste.

There seems, indeed, to have been a general desire on the part of the leaders of religious thought in India to follow the example of the great Buddha in his efforts to deliver the people from the tyranny of caste rules. At any rate they saw that the popularity of the doctrines they inculcated depended on their attracting adherents from all ranks, high and low. Hence, most of the great religious revivalists proclaimed the social equality of all who enrolled themselves in the same society, as worshippers of the same deity. But just as Buddhism ultimately fell back into Brāhmanism, so has every movement in the direction of equality and fraternity ended by a return, more or less complete, to the original condition of subjection to Brāhmanical authority and obedience to the law of caste distinctions.

In all likelihood the Brāhmanical revival under *Śankarāćārya* (to whom allusion has already been made) was nothing but a reaction towards caste. It probably originated in the desire of the Brāhmans to make some counter-demonstration against the Buddhistic movement. Śankara himself was a strict Brāhman and a great teacher of the Vedānta philosophy. He was therefore a strenuous upholder of the *Advaita* doctrine (see p. 83), and although his followers, who are very numerous in the South of India, sometimes call themselves Śaivas, they more generally style themselves *Smārtas*, as claiming to adhere strictly to *Smṛiti*. Śankara is said to have been a native of Kerala (Malabar), and to have flourished about the end of the 7th or beginning of the 8th century. He led an erratic, controversial life, and is thought by some to have inculcated the preferential worship of the god Śiva, as identified with the Supreme Being, of whom some declare him to have been an incarnation. Tradition also makes him the founder of a Śaiva sect of ascetics, called the Daśnāmī Daṇḍins, 'ten named mendicants,' so called because divided into ten classes.

Others again maintain that Śankara had a preference for Vaishṇavism. But, as a Vedantist, he really had no preference either for Śiva or Vishṇu. He is the reputed author of a vast number of treatises and commentaries on the Vedānta philosophy (including the *Ātma-bodha* and *Ānanda-laharī*). His learning and sanctity were in such repute that he was held to have worked various miracles; amongst others, animating the dead body of a king Amaru, so as to be able to argue with the wife of a Brāhman, named Mandana.[1]

Let us now notice briefly, and, if possible, in chronological order, six principal divisions of Vaishṇavism founded by leaders who lived at different epochs. They may be distinguished from each other by the names of their founders, thus,—

1. *The Nimbārkas.* 2. *The Rāmānujas.*
3. *The Madhvāćāryas.* 4. *The Rāmānandas.*
5. *The Vallabhāćāryas.* 6. *The C'aitanyas.*

Of course, the common link of all these sects is their belief in the supremacy of Vishṇu. Their difference consists in the character assigned to that god, in the practices and usages founded thereon by the leader to which each sect owes its origin, in the philosophical doctrines taught by that leader, and in distinctive sectarian marks (p. 98).

1. To begin with the Nimbārkas (vulgarly called *Nīmāndīs*), perhaps the least important of the six

[1] His object is supposed to have been to become the husband of the king's widow for a time, that he might learn by experience how to argue on amatory subjects with the wife of the Brāhman. This is described in the celebrated poem, *Amaru-śataka*, to which a mystical interpretation is given.

Vaishṇava sects, but the first in chronological order.

The founder's name was Nimbārka or Nimbāditya, and is generally supposed to have been identical with the astronomer, Bhāskarāćārya, who is thought to have flourished in the 12th century.

Others regard him as an actual incarnation of the Sun-god, undertaken for the revival of religion and the suppression of heresy.

The adherents of this sect possess few characteristic peculiarities. They worship Kṛishṇa and Rādhā conjointly, and their chief scriptural authority is the Bhāgavata-purāṇa (see p. 119). Although Nimbārka is said to have written a commentary on the Veda, this sect is not possessed of any literature of their own, the want of which they attribute to the destruction of their books at Mathurā, in the time of Aurangzīb.

This sect is distinguished by two perpendicular yellowish lines, made of Gopīćandana earth, drawn from the root of the hair to the commencement of each eyebrow, and there meeting in a curve, to represent the footprint of Vishṇu. A second curve is sometimes added below.

It should be noted here, that the poet Jayadeva, who is thought to have lived in the 12th century, may be said to have followed Nimbārka in promoting the doctrine of devotion to Kṛishṇa, by his celebrated poem called Gīta-govinda, in which are described the loves of Kṛishṇa and the Gopīs as typical of the longing of the human soul for union with the divine.[1]

---

[1] The late Dr. Adam Clarke appears to have been struck with the resemblance of this mystical poem to the Song of Solomon. See his Commentary.

2. The *Rāmānujas.*—These come next in order of time, and are a most important sect in the South of India.

They were founded by the celebrated reformer Rāmānuja, who was born at Śrī Parambattūr (about 26 miles west of Madras), and is known to have studied at Conjeveram, and to have resided at Śrī Rangam, near Trichinopoly. He probably flourished about the middle or latter part of the 12th century. The chief doctrine he promulgated was, that Vishṇu is the Supreme Being, that he was before all worlds, and was the cause and creator of all things.

This sect has two grand subdivisions:—1. The *Vadagalais*, or Northern School of Rāmānujas; 2. The *Tengalais*, or Southern School. The difference in their doctrines is something the same as that of Arminian and Calvinist. In philosophy they both belong to the Advaita, or non-dualistic school; but with this difference, that Rāmānuja, although he affirmed the ultimate oneness of man's soul with God's, declared that they could not be united in this life. This doctrine he called *Viśishṭ ādvaita.* One peculiarity of the sect consists in the scrupulous preparation and privacy of their meals. Another peculiarity of the Rāmānujas is that they never allow mustachios on the upper lip. Moreover, they often have the ćakra and other symbols of Vishṇu branded on their arms.

The frontal mark of both subdivisions of this sect consists of two perpendicular white lines drawn from the root of the hair to the commencement of each eyebrow, and meeting below in a curve. A central perpendicular reddish line is added to represent Lakshmī; and, in the case of the Tengalais, the white line is extended halfway down the nose, and the whole is supposed to represent the two feet of Vishṇu.

3. The *Mādhvas*, or *Madhvāčāryas*, are Vaishṇavas, but are not so important a sect as the last.

They were founded by the sage Madhva, or Madhvāčārya, otherwise called *Ānanda-tīrtha* and *Pūrṇa-prajna*, who was a strenuous opponent of Śankarāčārya's Advaita system of philosophy. He is said to have been born about the year 1200, and to have been educated in a convent at Ananteśvar.

Many of the disciples of this sect live in Maṭhas, or monasteries. Many of them are also simply philosophers, the school established by Madhva being called *Dvaita*, dualism, in opposition to the *A-dvaita* school, upheld by S'ankarāčārya, and followed by the Smārtas. The Dvaita school of Madhva asserts that God is supreme, yet essentially different from the human soul, and from the material world, both of which have a real and eternally distinct existence.

The frontal mark of this sect, who are chiefly found in the South of India, consists of two thin perpendicular lines meeting below in a curve, like those of the Rāmānujas, but the colour is red (instead of white), and the central perpendicular line is black, being generally made with the charcoal from incense burnt before the idols of Vishṇu.

4. The *Rāmānandas* (often called Rāmānandīs), are sometimes confounded with the Rāmānujas, from whom they differ very slightly. Indeed, Rāmānanda, the founder, was a disciple of Rāmānuja, and a teacher of substantially similar doctrines.

He flourished at Benares about the beginning of the 14th century. His followers are numerous in Gangetic India, especially around Agra. They worship Vishṇu under the form of Rāma-čandra with his consort Sītā. Their favourite work is the Bhakta-mālā, and their sectarian marks resemble those of the Rāmānujas. Their founder taught that all distinction of caste among the Vairāgīs and ascetic orders ought to be abolished.

Rāmānanda had twelve disciples, among whom the most celebrated was a remarkable reformer named Kabīr, who probably lived about the end of the 14th century.

This Kabīr became the founder of a distinct sect. He assailed idolatry with great boldness, and ridiculed the religious practices of his fellow-countrymen, though he allowed adoration to be paid to Vishṇu or Rāma, as names for one god. He promulgated a high moral code, declaring that life was a sacred gift of God, and that the blood of men or animals ought never to be shed by his creatures. He laid great stress on truthfulness, and advocated retirement from the world for the attainment of control over the passions.

It is supposed that Nānak Shah, the founder of the Sikh religion, who was born in the Panjāb, near Lahore, and in the reign of Bābar about the year 1500, attempted a compromise between Hindūism and Islām, was indebted to his predecessor Kabīr, for his pantheistic opinions, and some of the other ideas which characterize his system.[1] His order of ascetics (corresponding to Sannyāsīs and Vairāgīs), are called Udāsīs.

5. The *Vallabhāćāryas* form a very important sect in Bombay, Gujarāt, and Central India.

---

[1] The Ādi-grantha, 'first book,' which embodies his system, and is the bible of the Sikhs (prohibiting idol-worship, and teaching the unity of the Godhead pantheistically) was promulgated about the time of our Reformation.

Their founder, Vallabhāćārya, is said to have been born in the forest C'ampāraṇya in 1479, and is regarded by his followers as an incarnation of Kṛishṇa. Various miraculous stories are fabled about him. For instance, his intelligence is alleged to have been so great that when he commenced learning at the age of seven, he mastered the four Vedas, the six systems of Philosophy, and the eighteen Purāṇas in four months.

After such precocity we need not wonder that at the age of twelve he had formulated his teaching, and commenced travelling to propagate his doctrines. When he reached the court of Kṛishṇadeva, king of Vijayanagar, he was invited to a public disputation with the S'aivas, in which he succeeded so well that he was elected chief Āćārya of the Vaishṇavas. He then travelled for nine years through different parts of India, and finally settled in Benares, where he composed seventeen works; among which was the 'Bhāgavata-ṭīkā-subhodhinī,' or commentary on the Bhāgavata-purāṇa, which last work, especially its tenth book (see p. 107), is the chief authoritative source of the doctrines of the sect. In philosophy he maintained Vedāntist doctrines, and called his system *S'uddhādvaita*, 'pure non-dualism,' to distinguish it from the *Viśishtādvaita* of Rāmānuja. Vallabhāćārya died at Benares, or, according to his followers, was transported to heaven while performing his ablutions in the Ganges.

Vallabhāćārya left behind him eighty-four disciples who dispersed themselves throughout India and disseminated his doctrines. But the real successor to the Gādi (=*gaddī*) or Chair of Vallabhāćārya was his second son, Viṭṭhalnāth, sometimes called Gosāinjī from his having settled at Gokul, near Muttra (Mathurā). This Viṭṭhalnāth had seven sons, each of whom established a Gaddī in different parts of India, especially in Bombay, Kutch, Kāttiwār, and Malwa, and particularly among the merchants and traders called Ban:as and Bhatias. The influence of Vallabhācārya's successors became so great that they acquired the title of Mahārāja, the name Gosāin (for Gosvāmin—lord of cows—an epithet of Kṛishṇa) being sometimes added.

Vallabhācārya's system is called *Pushṭi-mārga*—'the way of eating, drinking, and enjoying oneself'; that is to say, worshipping the deity, not with fasting, self-denial, self-mortification, and penitence, but with indulgence of the natural appetites and enjoyment of the good things of the world. The god worshipped is the Kṛishṇa form of Vishṇu with his wives the Gopīs or cowherdesses. But their idol is generally one representing Kṛishṇa in his childhood, till his twelfth year. According to the purer Vaishṇava faith Kṛishṇa's love for the Gopīs, and especially for his favourite Rādhā, is to be explained allegorically, as symbolizing the longing of the human soul for the Supreme. But the Vallabhācāryas interpreted it in a gross and material sense. Hence their devotion to Kṛishṇa and his wives degenerated into the most corrupt practices, and their system became rotten to the core. Their men had brought themselves to believe that they must assimilate themselves to female Gopīs in doing homage to their god, and the Mahārājas or spiritual chiefs, the successors of Vallabhācārya, were to dress like women in order to commend themselves to Kṛishṇa.

But far more than this, these Mahārājas had come to be regarded as representatives of Kṛishṇa upon earth, and it was even believed by many that they were divine beings—incarnations of the god. Hence in the temples, where the Mahārājas did homage to the idols, men and women did homage to the Mahārājas, prostrating themselves at their feet, offering them incense, fruits, and flowers, and waving lights before them, as the Mahārājas themselves did before the images of the gods. One mode of worshipping the idols was by swinging them. Hence, women worshipped the Mahārājas by swinging them also in swings. The Pān-supārī ejected from their mouths and the leavings of their food were eagerly devoured by their devotees, who also drank the water rinsed from their garments, and called C'araṇāmṛita, 'feet nectar.'

But infinitely worse than all this—it was believed that the best mode of propitiating them was by ministering to their sensual appetites. Body, soul, and property (*tan, man, dhan*) were to be wholly made over to them by their disciples, and their women were taught to believe that highest bliss would be secured to themselves and their families by the caresses of Kṛishṇa's representatives.

It was this utter corruption of the Vaishṇava faith that led to a modern Puritan movement under a reformer Svāmi-Nārāyan, whose followers now number from 150,000 to 200,000 persons. They are chiefly found in Gujarāt, though a few are scattered here and there in the Deccan. Elsewhere in India they are unknown. They are presided over by two spiritual chiefs, the alleged successors of Svāmi-Nārāyan, and who like those of the Vallabhācāryas, are styled Mahārājas, their full title being, however, Mahārājādhirāja. One of them is settled at Wartāl, the other at Ahmedabad, the former taking the precedence, from the superior importance of the temple and monastery of which he is head.

Svāmi-Nārāyan, who took the name of Sahajānanda Svāmī (corrupted into Sejānanda), was not a native of Gujarāt. He was born in 1780 A.D., at Chapāi, a town in Oudh, about sixty kos to the north-east of Lucknow, and died about forty-six years ago, when he was forty-nine years old.

Living in Gujarāt, he soon became stirred in spirit by the sensuality of the Vallabhāćāryas. To counteract their licentious practices, Svāmi-Nārāyan, who, to a natural leaning towards *Udāsa* and asceticism, joined all the energy of a great reformer, made chastity and purity of life the keynote of all his teaching,[1] and ended by boldly asserting that he himself, and not Vallabhāćārya, was the true incarnation of Kṛishṇa, and that the god, in order to restore the Vaishṇava faith to its former purity, had descended in his person as a Brahmaćārī, or Brāhman under a vow of continence.

6. *The C'aitanyas.* This sect is peculiar to Bengal and Orissa, where it is of great importance and well known.

The founder, C'aitanya, was born about 1485, and regarded as an incarnation of Kṛishṇa. At the age of twenty-four he became an ascetic, and travelled to Jagannāth, in Orissa, where he taught Vaishṇava doctrines.

He remained twelve years at Katak, engaged in intense medi-

[1] Their code of instructions is of a very pure and lofty character. It is comprised in a little work called *S'ikshā-patrī*, a copy of which, with a commentary in Gujarātī and Sanskṛit, was presented to me by the Mahārāja of Wartāl on the occasion of my visit to the temple and monastery at that place, over which he presides.

tation on Kṛishṇa. But this was not his only occupation. He insisted on the importance of singing (*sankīrtana*) and dancing, as well as of contemplation, to fit the mind for ecstatic communion with the deity, and his followers often swooned away in their fits of religious emotion. He was himself subject to fits of religious ecstasy, and died during one of them whilst bathing in the sea near Purī. After his death he was canonized, and declared to have been an incarnation of Kṛishṇa.

C'aitanya's disciples soon spread themselves over Bengal. They hold that Kṛishṇa is the Supreme Being, and that *bhakti* or faith in him is more efficacious than knowledge, than subjugation of the passions, than meditation (*yoga*), than charity, virtue, or anything usually deemed most meritorious. All castes become by such faith equally pure, and all castes are equally admissible into the sect. Their chief ritual consists in constantly repeating the name Kṛishṇa. A great many treatises have been written in support of their tenets, which are highly esteemed in Bengal.

Besides the above-described six principal sects of Vaishṇavas, there are many others of less importance; such as the followers of *Viṭhṭhal* or *Viṭho-bā* (a form of Kṛishṇa)[1] worshipped more especially at Paṇḍharpur in Mahā-rāshṭra, and the favourite of the celebrated Marāṭhī poet Tukārāma; the followers of *Dādū* (*Dādū-pathins*), a famous ascetic who lived at Jaipur about A.D. 1600; the *Mīrabāīs* a subdivision of the Vallabhāćāryas founded by Mīrābāī, the wife of the Rāna of Udaipur; and several others.

[1] The images of this form of Kṛishṇa generally represent him and his wife with their hands resting on their hips.

With regard to the so-called Śaiva sects, there are a large number of Śaivas in the South of India, called *Linga-vats* (commonly Lingā-its and Jangamas), as wearing the Linga on their persons. They were founded by a leader named Vṛishabha, who taught the suppression of all caste distinctions, and the uselessness of all Brāhmanical rites. This sect bury instead of burning their dead. Another so called Śaiva sect, the *Pāśupatas* (worshippers of Siva in his character of *Paśu-pati*, lord of the soul, called *paśu*), base their philosophical doctrines on a system called Śiva-siddhānta.

Śaiva ascetics are properly called Sannyāsīs, but they are often confounded with other orders of ascetics, called Vairāgīs (supposed to be properly Vaishṇavas), Gosāins, Yogīs, &c. The following are other orders :—

The *Paramahansas*, or the highest order of Yogīs, who are solely occupied with meditating on Brahmā ;[1] the *Aghorins* or *Aghora-pathins*, who propitiate S'iva by revolting austerities ; the *Ūrdhva-bāhus*, who extend one or both arms over the head and hold them in that position for years ; the *Ākāśa-mukhins*, who keep their necks bent back looking up at the sky ; the *Daṇḍins*, or mendicant staff-bearers, a subdivision of whom has been already described as founded by S'ankarācārya (see p. 137).

Having thus noted the principal divisions of Vaishṇavas and Śaivas, which owe their origin to the great leaders of religious thought and practice in medieval and modern times, we cannot conclude this

[1] This is the highest order of ascetics. The theory is that a Yogī who aims at perfection ought to go through six courses of austerity of twelve years each. In the last he is called a *Parama-hansa*.

part of our subject without glancing at the opinions of the Brāhmas, or members of the various modern theistical societies (Samājas) now springing up in various parts of India. Their first founder was a well-known Brāhman, named Rāja Rām Mohun Roy, a man of great ability, born near Burdwan, in 1774. He was the first Hindū reformer that arose after the establishment of the British Ṛāj in India.

Besides exerting himself for the abolition of Satī (commonly called Suttee, or the burning of Indian widows with their deceased husbands), and the promo tion of native education, he preached everywhere pure monotheism, endeavouring to prove that the idolatry of the Hindūs was contrary to the practice of their ancestors, and to the precepts of the Veda; but he used the Indian name Brahma for the Supreme Being, and called the society he founded the *Brahma-samāj*, or Society of God. Its doctrines were in fact founded on a monotheistic interpretation of the Veda.

After the death of Rām Mohun Roy, his friend Dvāraka Nāth Tagore, a man of great weight and influence, gave his support to the Brahma-samāj, but it languished without a leader till his son Debendra Nāth Tagore formed the nucleus of a new community, now called the Ādi Samāj, or first church. This society publicly renounced idolatry, and declared their belief in the one God as defined in the Vedānta. Then a third great leader arose, Keshab C'andra Sen who has recently visited England. He rejects entirely the Hindū system, including the Vedānta. His society is called the Progressive or New Samāj (*Nūtana*). Their creed may be described as "a belief in the Fatherhood of God, and the Brotherhood of mankind," and its theology might be well expressed by the first part of the first Article of the Church of England: "There is but one living and true God—everlasting, without body, parts, or passions, of infinite power, wisdom and goodness, the maker and preserver of all things."

Other forms of theistical Samāj exist in India; for example, one called the Prārthanā Samāj or *Prayer Society*, at Bombay. These have the Vedānta formula *Ekam evādvitīyam* (see p. 11) inscribed over the entrance to their house of prayer, recently erected. Moreover, a new Brāhman reformer named Dayānanda, has recently appeared, and is attracting many adherents in the West of India. He is engaged in writing a new commentary to the Ṛig-veda, which he interprets monotheistically, and his society is called the Ārya-samāj.

We must acknowledge with thankfulness the good these theistical societies are doing by their uncompromising opposition to idolatry, fanaticism, superstition, and caste. They are the present protestants of India.

Nevertheless it is to be feared that, with the exception of the Progressive Samāj of Calcutta, they are not altogether free from a suspicion of pantheistic proclivities.

CHAPTER XI.

MODERN CASTES.

NOTWITHSTANDING the constant efforts of great religious leaders in India to deliver their fellow-countrymen from the tyranny of caste, the power of caste has always in the end recovered its ascendency. It might almost indeed be inferred from the influence exerted by caste-rules on the daily life of the Hindūs that the whole of their religion was centred in caste-observances, and that Hindūism and caste were convertible terms. And, in point of fact, strictness in the maintenance of caste is the only real test of Hindūism exacted by the Brāhmans of the present day. In matters of mere faith, Hindūism is (as we have seen) all-tolerant and all-receptive. No person who is not born a Brāhman can become one, but any person can be admitted into the lower ranks of Hindūism who will acknowledge the supremacy of the Brāhmans and obey the rules of caste. So long as a man holds to his caste, he is at liberty to hold any opinions he likes, even to accepting the doctrines of Christianity.

> Perfection is alone attained by him
> Who swerves not from the business of his caste.[1]

Caste, as a social institution, exists, of course, in

[1] See the Bhagavad-Gītā, quoted in the appendix of this volume (p. 209).

all countries, and in England operates with no slight potency. We believe in a close connection between blood and breeding; and, although we do not go so far as to hold that different grades of society have different coloured skins (according to the original Hindū theory), yet we have a difficulty in admitting that a man who is not a gentleman by birth can ever be made one by training. With us, however, caste is not a religious institution. On the contrary, our religion, though it sanctions differences of rank, teaches us that class-distinctions ought to be laid aside in the worship of God, and that there is no respect of persons with Him. Nor with us does caste prevent a certain amount of social union, intercourse, interchange of ideas, and even intermarriage, between the various classes of society; nor does it, as in India, operate to merge the individual in the corporate body, to set class against class, to prevent the lower rising to the upper, and to make national union impossible. On the contrary, with us all ranks and orders so run into each other and blend imperceptibly together, that it becomes impossible to separate them into sharply-defined strata, or to say where the upper ends and the middle or lower begins.

Very different is the caste theory of the Hindūs. The doctrine of Manu was (see pp. 57, 58) that the deity created distinct kinds of men, as he created varieties of animals; and that Brāhmans, Kshatriyas, Vaiśyas, and Śūdras were born and must remain from birth to death distinct from each other. A Brāhman, however, could have four wives, and marry a woman belonging to any of the three lower castes. Intermarriage could also take place between members of all the four classes, or again, between the mixed castes which resulted from such intercourse. In this way it happened that, although no man could himself enter a caste higher or lower than his own, he might by the act of marriage lead to the formation of a new mixed caste, to which a distinct occupation was assigned. It was thus, in fact, that new mixed castes were constantly created, and even castes of the lowest grade were derived from the highest by occasional perpetration of what was held to be a great abomination—the marriage of a Śūdra father with a woman of a superior caste. For example, a *C'aṇḍāla*, or hunter of animals, living in holes, who was the most degraded of mortals and not allowed to perform Śrāddhas for his own ancestors, had a Brāhman mother and Śūdra father; and the *Āyogava*, or carpenter, who was also utterly despised, was half Vaiśya, half Śūdra. Again, the *Sva-pāka*, dog-feeder, who was a public executioner and compelled to live outside villages, was half Kshatriya, half Śūdra.

The only caste that has retained its purity to any extent is that of the Brāhmans, though examples of pure Kshatriyas may be found among the Rājputs, and some pure Vaiśyas probably exist among the Baniahs, or traders and shopkeepers. Moreover, instead of Manu's mixed castes,—arising from the permissible intermarriage of the pure castes,—we have an almost endless number of what may be called trade-castes, resulting chiefly from associations of men engaged in the same occupations,—which are being constantly created, and in which exclusiveness and restrictions in regard to social intercourse and intermarriage are enforced far more strictly than in the original pure castes of ancient times. Many of these trade-unions resemble the guilds of artisans once common in Europe, and have numerous sub-castes under them.[1] Each society keeps aloof from the other, and shuts itself up in its own independence. And yet, within each caste, individual independence is impossible, because no individual can act alone, but only in conjunction with his caste-fellows.

Probably, the original idea of caste was, that difference of complexion, or skin-colour (*varṇa*), marked a natural separation between the grades of society. The early immigrants found parts of India occupied by Negroid aborigines, almost as dark as Africans; and they themselves, by intermarriage with the primitive tribes (some of them afterwards called Śūdras), and again by further intermarriage among themselves, lost their original fairness of complexion. Hence subsequent immigrants arriving in India, and finding those already settled there as cultivators of the soil (*vaiśyas*) more dark-coloured than themselves, claimed a superiority of rank based upon greater purity of blood, which purity, they believed, could only be maintained by strict prohibitions against intermarriage with the lower classes. We may in this way account for the origin of the higher castes of Brāhmans and Kshatriyas. Soon a theory was advanced that food had an important effect on the preservation of blood-purity, and strict regulations about eating and drinking came into force. As time went on, still further safeguards were elaborated.

[1] In the North-west, the Kāyasth, or writer caste, has twelve subdivisions, and similarly, the Barhaī, or carpenter caste, has seven sub-castes, none of which can eat together.

Even contact with the skin of persons of inferior caste was thought likely to cause contamination. Hence, only men of the same caste were allowed to eat together and work together; and when a death occurred, no man could be carried to the burning-ground except by his own caste-fellows. These rules have multiplied almost endlessly among the almost endless divisions of modern caste; but it will be observed that, however numerous and intricate such rules have become, they still affect a man chiefly in the four matters of marriage, food, professional occupation, and funeral rites.

As to the first of these, intermarriage between different castes, which in Manu's time was permissible is now altogether prohibited, and a kind of *endogamy*, or marriage within a limited circle of caste-associates, leading to many objectionable results, is enforced, not only in each caste, but even generally in every sub-caste. For example, there are, it is said, eighty-four sub-castes of Brāhmans in Gujarāt which are not allowed to intermarry, and in many of these there are more males than females.[1]

In regard to the second point, of 'food,' the rules are more strict than in Manu's time, not merely as to the kind of food, but also as to the mode of its preparation, and the persons with whom it is eaten. All the higher classes agree in abstaining from animal food, the eating of which, although formerly permitted on certain occasions, is now regarded as a sin. Again,

[1] The sub-castes of the Kāyasths cannot intermarry except with the highest of the twelve.

all classes, high and low, hold it to be not only a sin, but an act of downright impiety, to eat the flesh of oxen.[1] Even to sit in the presence of an Englishman while engaged in eating beef, is not only sinful, but produces feelings of disgust far greater than an Englishman would feel in sitting next to a Chinaman while satisfying his appetite with a meal of boiled rats. The sacredness and inviolability of the cow and ox is in real truth a universally applicable test of modern orthodox Hindūism.

So also it is not merely a breach of social propriety, but an offence against religion, for a man of high caste to eat food prepared by one of inferior caste; or for members of different castes to eat together.[2] An important distinction, however, in regard to eating together is made between food cooked with water and dry food. The former consists of boiled rice, dāl, &c., or of coarse baked cakes, and this kind of food, which contains no ghī, is eaten by all castes apart from each other, after washing their hands and feet, and removing part of their clothing. On the other hand, dry food comprehends not only all dry eatables and fruit, but also food cooked with ghī, as well as

---

[1] Happily for the Hindūs, the cow which supplies them with their only animal food—milk and butter—and the ox, which helps to till their ground, were declared sacred at an early period. Had it not been so, this useful animal might have been exterminated in times of famine. What is now a superstition had its origin, like some other superstitions, in a wise foresight.

[2] Contrast St. Paul, 1 Cor. v. 11—"Now I have written unto you not to keep company, if any man that is called a brother be a fornicator, or covetous, or an idolater, or a railer, or a drunkard, or an extortioner; with such an one no not to eat."

sweetmeats; and this may be eaten without removing any garments, without washing, and in company with other castes.

To understand the process by which such ideas have acquired strength, and become absolutely dominant, it may be well to bear in mind that every Hindū has a tendency to confuse the relationship between matter and spirit. Indian philosophers assert that matter is illusory, or that it has no real existence distinct from spirit, which is the only true entity.[1] Hence a Hindū is convinced that inanimate material substances may be animated with powerful spiritual forces, and that such forces may exert a mysterious influence on the well-being of the immaterial part of his nature. It is therefore more important that water and food should be religiously than chemically pure. Every orthodox Hindū is perfectly persuaded that the dirtiest water, if taken from a sacred stream and applied to his body, either externally or internally, will purify his soul. Consequently he will either bathe in it or drink it with avidity; whereas the purest water is supposed to cause external and internal taint if accepted from a person of low caste. Similarly he believes that the purest food if touched by a person of low caste, or by a European (*Mleċċha*) will, if eaten, contaminate his blood, and that such contamination will affect his character and prospects in this world and the next. Even the approach of a person of low caste, or no caste, or his shadow falling on food during its preparation, is

[1] There is no proper philosophical word in Sanskṛit for matter, unless it be *jaḍa*, opposed to *ċetana* spirit.

thought to impart a taint which makes the most wholesome meal unfit to be eaten.

With regard to the third point affected by caste, viz. professional pursuits, it should be observed that Brāhmans alone are allowed free liberty of engaging in the occupations of other castes. Formerly only six acts were permitted to a strict Brāhman, viz., repetition of the Veda (*adhyayana*), teaching it to others (*adhyāpana*), sacrificing (*yajana*), assisting at sacrifices (*yājana*), giving (*dāna*), and receiving gifts (*pratigraha*). But even in Manu's time Brāhmans might under certain circumstances become soldiers, or live by agriculture, keeping cattle, or trade (Manu, x. 80–82, 101, 102; ix. 319). In the present day they are often cooks, and they may engage in any industrial arts not involving contamination and degradation.

The other castes are generally restricted to one occupation, but the names of the castes are not always a guide to the nature of their employments, these latter having sometimes in process of time become changed.

Indeed it is by opening its arms to receive associations of men engaged in the same art or trade that Hindūism, which is not in theory a proselyting creed, is continually extending itself. Any body of men, pursuing the same occupation, may form themselves into a kind of trade-union, and the Brāhmans will admit them into the pale of their religion, the sole conditions being that they bind themselves not to intermarry with other castes, and accept the supremacy of the Brāhmans and the sacredness of the cow or ox.

The fourth and last point affected by caste, is the performance of funeral rites, and of Śrāddhas in honour of the dead. This interesting subject has been already noticed (see p. 65). We have only space to state further that considerable variation in the performance of such ceremonies prevails everywhere throughout India, and that all diversities of usage in this matter depend upon difference of caste, and of sub-caste, and even sometimes of groups of families.

It only remains for us to enumerate some of the more important divisions and subdivisions of caste now found in India.[1]

To begin with the Brāhmans who are still religiously above all other castes, and are still in their own estimation, and in that of bigoted Hindūs, the 'lords of creation' by a kind of divine right. They are divided into ten principal tribes, thus:

The northern division of Brāhmans (sometimes called *Gauḍa*) has five tribes under it, according to the proper abode, viz., the *Kānyakubja* (Kanauj), *Sārasvata* (North-west), *Gauḍa* (Bengal and Delhi), *Maithila* (North Behar), *Utkala* (Orissa). The southern division (called *Drāviḍa*) has also five; viz., the *Mahārāshṭra* (Marāṭhī districts), *Tailinga* (Telugu), *Drāviḍa* (Tamil), *Karṇāṭa* (Karnatic), and *Gurjara* (Gujarāt). The first tribe of the northern division, viz. the *Kānyakubja*, or Kanauj, is again numerously subdivided, and especially into one hundred and fifty-six tribes, of which one hundred are called *Vārendra*, and fifty-six *Rāḍha* or *Rāṛh* (from Rāḍhā, a district in the west of Bengal). Of the former, eight, and of the latter six, are regarded as *Kulīna*, or noble. The six Kulīna Rāṛh tribes are Banerjea, Mukhurjea, C'aturjea, Gārguli, Goshāla, and Kanjalāla.

[1] The Rev. M. A. Sherring, of Benares, has published a useful work on this subject, which is my chief authority here.

Again, all tribes of Brāhmans are divided into *Gotras* or groups of families, according as they are supposed to be derived from one or other of the seven mythical sages, Bhṛigu, Angiras, Atri, Viśvāmitra, (Kauśika), Kaśyapa, Vaśishṭha, and Agastya. These seven sets of Gotras are again subdivided into others too numerous to mention.[1]

Again, Brāhmans are still further classified according to their supposed particular line of study, or extent of learning; as, for example, whether a man knows the Ṛig-veda alone (*Ṛigveda-śākhī*), or the Yajur-veda (*Yajurveda-śākhī*), or two Vedas (*dvi-vedī*, commonly called Dobe), or three Vedas (*tri-vedī*, commonly Tiverī), or four Vedas (*ćatur-vedī* commonly Chaube), or some particular branch (*S'ākhā*) of one of the Vedas or its Sūtras, or whether he is generally a learned man (*Paṇḍita*). Other titles are the result of difference of occupation; as, for instance,—

The *S'rotriya* who performs Vedic ceremonies; the *Yājnika*, who performs the Sanskāras; the *Vaidika*, who recites the Veda; the *S'āstrī* who explains the law-books; the *Paurāṇika* who recites the Purāṇas; the *Jyotisha*, who knows astronomy, and settles the calendar; the *Mahā-brāhmaṇa* or *Mahā-pātra* (in some places called *Āćārya*), who arranges the ceremonies at times of death and mourning; the *Gangā-putra*, who sits near the Ganges and guides the pilgrims at Benares; the *Gayā-wāl*, who superintends the pilgrims at Gayā; the *Prayāg-wāl*, who does the same at Allahābād; the *Ojhā*—exorciser of demons; the last five of whom are Brāhmans of an inferior order, and some are regarded with contempt by high-caste Brāhmans.

The Rājputs, who represent the ancient Kshatriya, military and royal caste, and come next to the Brāhmans, are also divided into numerous tribes or clans,

[1] There are eighty-four subdivisions in Gujarāt alone.

too numerous to be detailed. The original occupation of this caste was twofold—that of governing and that of fighting, and even now many of the soldiers in our Sepoy (*sipāhī*) regiments are Rājputs, while even with the spread of British power, a few Rājput princes remain in India, and are permitted to retain a certain amount of kingly authority. We may instance as examples, the Mahārājas of Udaipur, Jodhpur, Jaipur, Rewah, Bikanīr. These claim to belong to the ancient Solar dynasty (*S'ūrya-vanśa*). Others, such as the Mahārājas of Jaisalmīr and Karowlī, claim to be descended from the Lunar line (*Soma-vanśa*).

A less pure order of Kshatriyas are the *Jats* or *Jāts* (not properly entitled to the name of Rājput), who are numerous in Rājputāna and the Panjāb. At the head of them comes the Mahārāja of Bhartpur. They are often great landowners, and often they and the Rājputs are simple agriculturists. They have numerous sub-divisions. Other clans allied to them are the Gūjars, who are also generally agriculturists. Perhaps, however, one of the chief tribes of agriculturists and tillers of the soil is a mixed class called *Kumbī* (or *Kuṇbī*, or *Kurmī*, probably connected with Sanskṛit root *kṛish*), extensively found over large districts of Hindūstān proper and Central India.

It is clear, therefore, that even Rājputs, Jats, and other modern castes may represent the ancient Vaiśyas, who were originally the great class of agriculturists —the men who settled down (root *viś*) on the soil as husbandmen and cultivators. In fact, very few of the

---

[1] They claim to be descended from Kṛishṇa, of the Yadu branch of the Lunar line.

present so-called Vaiśya caste have anything to do with agriculture. Some of them may be of tolerably pure descent, but they are generally merchants, shopkeepers, and traders, forming tribes called Banias or Baniyas (Sanskṛit *baṇik*), Bhātiyas, &c., many of whom are Vaishṇavas, and many Jains in their creed. A large class of traders are called *Khatrīs*, which name probably shows that they are descended from the ancient Kshatriyas, and in certain privileges, such as that of wearing the sacred thread (commonly called *Janeo=yajnopavīta*), and repeating the Gāyatrī and parts of the Veda, these Khatrī traders who are often shopkeepers, dealers in cloth, silk, lace, &c., come nearer to the ancient Kshatriyas than the Rājputs, who claim to represent them.[1]

Other important classes of traders who claim Vaiśya descent are the *Agarwālās* of North-western and Central India (mostly Jains in religion),—the *Oswāls* of Gujarāt (also found at Benares), the *Bandarwārs*, the *Rastogīs*, the *Banjārās* (wandering merchants), &c. The above mercantile and trading communities constitute the most enterprising and enlightened, as well as the best-educated of all the Indian castes (not excepting the Brāhmans), and it is from this source that a strong middle-class capable of creating and fostering a sound healthy public opinion—one of the greatest of India's needs—may one day be derived.

Another enterprising and educated class are called

---

[1] Rājput boys also wear the sacred cord, but they are not invested with it till marriage, whereas the Khatrīs receive it at eight years of age. In some parts of India, Kathaks (musicians), Sūtārs (carpenters), Sonārs (goldsmiths), Bhātiyas and Kaserās (braziers), also wear the Janeo.

Kāyasthas or writers, who claim to have had a Brāhman progenitor named C'itra-gupta. They come next in rank to the Vaiśya or trading communities, and are by some affirmed to be pure Śūdras, though they are much above those lower classes now called Śūdras. The members of this caste (who are often vulgarly called Kaits) discharge most important duties in the government law-courts and other offices. They are lawyers, clerks, accountants, keepers of registers, &c., and are generally most intelligent and well-informed.

There are at least twelve sub-castes of Kāyasthas, divided in Bengal into eleven clans, named Gos (*ghosha*), Bose (*vasu*), Mitra, De, Datt, Kor, Pālit, Das, Sen, Singh, Guha. Furthermore, in Bengal there is a caste called *Vaidya* or *Baidya*, 'medical' (=*Ambashṭha*, Manu, x. 8), which comes next in rank to the Brāhman.

It will not be possible for us to enumerate all the castes formed by associations of men engaged in various employments, trades, arts, industrial and menial occupations. Some of the commonest are the following—

Bhāts or *C'arans*, reciters of poetry at weddings, &c. (or in praise of Rājput princes, &c.); *Kathaks*, professional musicians (these play on various musical instruments and teach singing and dancing to prostitutes, for no respectable women either sing or dance, and even bad women seldom play on instruments); *Sonārs* (*suvarṇa-kāra*), goldsmiths, a subdivision of whom are the *Ratha-kāras*, who claim to be a Brāhman race; *Lohārs* (*loha-kāra*), blacksmiths; *Baṛhaīs* or *Sūtārs* (*sūtra-dhāra*), carpenters, sometimes employed as smiths; *Tantīs* (*tantrin*), weavers, who also manufacture Kim-khāb (properly the Persian *Kam-khwāb*, and vulgarly Kinkob), or cloth interwoven with gold and silver thread (there is also a weaver caste called *Kolīs*); *Kaserās* (*kansa-kāra*), braziers or workers in brass, copper, &c. ; *Telīs* (*tailin*), oilmen ; *Kumbhārs* or Kumhārs (*Kumbha-kāra*), potters ; *Dhobīs* (*dhāvaka*), washermen, (no Hindū, however poor, washes his own clothes ; this operation must be performed by the Dhobī caste, who are generally known by their donkeys) ; *Mālīs*, gardeners ; *Loṇārīs* (*lavaṇa-kārin*), preparers of salt ; *Rangārīs* (*ranga-kārin*), dyers ; *Halwāīs*, confectioners ; *Dirzīs*, tailors (who, when Muhammadans, are euphemistically called Khalīfas or Caliphs) ; *Nāūs* (*nāpita*) or *Hajjāms*, barbers (who are also go-betweens in arranging marriages) ; *Ahīrs*, herdsmen ; *Kahārs*, palankin-bearers ; *Mallāhs*, boatmen ; *Pāśīs*, village watchmen. To the above may be added unclean castes, such as *Camār* (*carma-kāra*) or *Mocīs*, leather-cutters and shoemakers ; *Mihtars* or *Bhangīs*, sweepers or scavengers ; *Doms*, cane chair-makers (these are the lowest of the low ; they are often employed as street-sweepers and in furnishing wood and fire for the burning of dead bodies) ; *Kūlīs*, labourers ; this last name is rather applicable to any labourer than to a caste, being derived from a Drāviḍian word, and meaning 'one who receives (daily) wages or *kūli*.'

It is satisfactory to know that, although it is too true that caste is still the very life and soul of Hindūism, and although this very caste is not without certain good points and advantages, yet some of its most vexatious rules are gradually giving way under the pressure of steam, electricity, and European influence. Many years ago a Brāhman who accidentally touched leather would have had to choose between public expiation or degradation, and expulsion from caste, whereas in 1870 a Uriya Brāhman held the post of sub-inspector of police in Purī itself, within the very shadow of Jagannāth, although a leather belt formed part of his uniform.[1]

[1] Hunter's Orissa, vol. ii. p. 147.

CHAPTER XII.

MODERN IDOL-WORSHIP, SACRED OBJECTS, HOLY PLACES AND TIMES.

No account of Hindūism can pretend to completeness without some notice of its modern idol-worship, and of its numerous minor deities, semi-divine beings, consecrated objects, holy places, and seasons.

Hindūism assigns no limit to the ever-increasing number of its deified existences, and we may safely affirm that there is no country in the world where so many shrines dedicated to gods and goddesses under different forms, images, symbols, and names, meet the eye as in India. In large towns temples are reckoned by hundreds, and even by thousands.

First, there are temples to the principal deities described in the previous chapters of this volume—to Śiva and his symbol (the linga), to Vishṇu, to Kṛishṇa, to Rāma, and to their respective wives—Durgā, Lakshmī, Rādhā, Sītā, under different forms and names. Then, there are occasional shrines containing images of divine heroes, such as Yudhishṭhira, Arjuna, Bhīma (see p. 112), and of divine Ṛishis, such as Bharadvāja, &c. Everywhere are seen images of the god Gaṇeśa, or *Gaṇapati*, son of Śiva and Durgā. He is lord of the troops of mischievous and malignant imps who are supposed to cause obstacles and difficulties, and is therefore invoked at the commencement of all undertakings. His bloated, dwarfish, and distorted appearance, which is like that of the Gaṇas of Śiva over whom he presides, indicates sensuality and love of good living, while his elephant's head is said to typify a combination of wisdom, or, perhaps, rather, of cunning and sagacity.

Again, shrines to the other son of Śiva, Skanda or Kārttikeya, the leader or general of Śiva's armies or troops of demons, are very common in the south of India. He is there called Subrahmaṇya.

Next are found all over India shrines dedicated to the Monkey-god Hanumān, the devoted ally of the great Rāma in his conflict with the Rākshasas of the South of India (see p. 111). His images are smeared with the sacred colour vermilion, to denote the estimation in which he is held, and the universal admiration of his devotion as a model faithful servant. After the great war, and the subjugation of Rāvaṇa, king of Ceylon, Rāma is said to have made over to Hanumān a great portion of the Deccan (*i.e.* Dakshiṇa, or south country, sometimes called Rāma-kshetra, and sometimes Daṇḍakāraṇya), of which Hanumān and his followers became the principal colonizers. Hence idols of the monkey-leader are found in (and often outside) every village of the Marāṭhī country.

Then in some towns, such as Benares, besides the principal shrines there are temples of the *Nava-grahāḥ*, nine planets, that is of the Sun-god (Sūrya), Moon-god (C'andra), Mars, Mercury, Jupiter, Venus, Saturn, Rāhu (dragon's-head, or ascending node of the moon, and cause of eclipses), and Ketu (dragon'stail), which, with the Nakshatras (see p. 180), constitute a formidable galaxy of deities whose favour must be conciliated before marriages and other auspicious events can be successfully accomplished,—with many special shrines, such as those of *Anna-pūrṇā*, the goddess of plenty; *S'ītalā*, the goddess of small-pox; *Bhairava-nātha* or *Daṇḍa-pāṇi*, a sort of deified police magistrate, and others too numerous to describe.

Again, carved stone images of the following well-known deities of the Hindū Pantheon are not uncommon:—

Indra, god of the atmosphere; *Varuṇa*, god of the ocean; *Kuvera*, god of wealth; *Kāma*, god of love; *Bala-rāma*, the Hindū Hercules; *Paraśu-rāma*, a deified Brāhman who is especially connected with the Konkan (called from him *Paraśurāma-kshetra*) and sometimes regarded as the god of the Konkanastha Brāhmans; *Yama*, god and judge of the dead.

But shrines dedicated to their honour are unusual.[1]

Nor are certain groups (*gaṇa*) of gods honoured with special shrines. The following, however, are reverenced:—

The ten *Viśva-devas*; the eight *Vasus* (forms of fire or light); the eleven *Rudras* (see p. 25); the twelve *Ādityas* (see p. 23); the *Sādhyas*, celestial beings of peculiar purity; the *Siddhas*, semi-divine beings of great perfection.

But the idol-worship of the towns by no means represents the common cultus of the rural districts of India. No village is too small, no locality too little frequented to be without its own peculiar religious symbols. At the tops of hills, in groves, on every

---

[1] I have never met with shrines to Indra, Varuṇa, Kuvera, or Yama, though their images often stand in the galleries of temples, or are carved on *the walls of caves*.

high place, and almost under every rock and stately tree, are to be seen, if not finished temples, at least rough idols or simple blocks of stone and wood, consecrated to local deities by patches of red paint, and bearing witness to the belief of the inhabitants in the presence of presiding gods and goddesses. There is, in truth, a strange mixture of aboriginal fetishism with Brāhmanical pantheism in the popular religion of the mass of the Hindū people. Everything great and useful — everything strange, monstrous, and unusual, whether good or evil, is held to be permeated by the presence of divinity. It is not merely all the mighty phenomena and forces of the universe—all the most striking manifestations of almighty energy—that excite the awe and attract the reverence of the ordinary Hindū. There is not an object in earth or heaven which he is not prepared to worship—rocks, stocks, and stones, trees, pools, and rivers, his own implements of trade,[1] the animals he finds most useful, the noxious reptiles he fears, men remarkable for any extraordinary qualities,—for great valour, sanctity, virtue, or even vice; good and evil demons, ghosts and goblins, the spirits of departed ancestors, an infinite number of semi-human, semi-divine existences—inhabitants of the seven upper and the seven lower worlds—each and all of these come in for a share of divine honour or a tribute of more or less adoration. Verily, the Hindū Pantheon has a place for everybody and

[1] Every trade, profession, and calling has its tutelary divinity. Even the Thugs claimed the goddess Kālī as their presiding goddess, in whose honour they murdered their victims.

everything. The deities already described are merely the occupants of its most conspicuous niches. To attempt an exhaustive enumeration of its minor gods and goddesses would be a hopeless task, and to count the ever-multiplying army of its martyrs, saints, and sages, would be a simple impossibility. New shrines are continually springing up to receive the remains of holy men or ascetics—examples of extraordinary sanctity, or of some peculiar manifestation of the divine energy—who, after death, are canonized and deified.[1]

With regard to animals, plants, and stones, we can only indicate those most generally revered.

Of all animals the cow is the most sacred. It typifies the all-yielding earth. It is the chief source of nourishment of every Hindū. All agricultural labour depends on the ox, for no such animal as a cart-horse exists in India. There is a typical 'cow of plenty' (*Kāma-dhenu*)—supposed to yield all desired objects—images of which are commonly sold in the bazaars, and bought as objects of reverence; and the letting loose of a bull (*vṛishctsarga*)—properly stamped with the symbol of Śiva—in sacred cities like Benares and Gayā, that it may be tended and reverenced by pious persons, is a highly meritorious act.

Serpents, also, are divine animals; they are emblematical of eternity, and are often associated with the gods, especially Siva. Moreover, a curious

[1] Such men are generally buried, not burnt, and their tombs resorted to by hundreds of pilgrims. Tombs containing the ashes of Satīs, or women who have burnt themselves with the bodies of their deceased husbands, are also common everywhere in India, and greatly revered.

race of serpents, half human, half divine, called Nāgas, is supposed to exist in the regions under the earth. They are ruled over by three principal serpents, named *S'esha*, *Vāsuki*, and *Takshaka*. According to some, this serpent race, however fabulous, points to the former existence of a class of beings to which the serpent that tempted Eve may have belonged, before the sentence was pronounced by which it became a creeping reptile.

Monkeys, a whole army of which aided Rāma in his conquest of Ceylon, are, of course, among the most sacred of all animals. They are inviolable, and never under any circumstances to be molested. Swarms of them are encouraged to infest the vicinity of temples and consecrated buildings, where they subsist on the food offered to them by pious worshippers.

But not only animal life, plant life also is held sacred, because thought to be permeated by divinity. Perhaps the Tulsī plant (properly *Tulasī*), or holy Basil, is the most revered. It is sacred to Vishṇu, and even prayers are addressed to it, as if it were itself a goddess. The marriage of the Tulsī with the god Vishṇu, or Kṛishṇa, is celebrated in every Hindū family in the month Kārttik.

So also the Vilva (Bel) tree, with its triple leaf, is sacred to Śiva, with his triple functions.

The Pīpal tree (*Ficus religiosa*) is another divine tree. It is regarded as occupied by the god Brahmā, and is sometimes invested with the sacred thread as if it were a real person. All the ceremonies of Upanayana are then performed over it.

No native will willingly cut down a Tulsī plant, or

a Pīpal tree, and the planting of these is always considered a religious and meritorious act.

The Aśoka shrub is also sacred to Śiva; the Dūrbā grass to Gaṇeśa; the Banyan tree to Kāla or Time; the Arka plant to Sūrya or the Sun. The Śamī or Acacia is a goddess on her own account, and is supposed to contain fire. The Custard-apple is called the fruit of Sītā (*sītā-phala*). The Kuśa is a most sacred grass.

Then as to stones. Black stones, called Śālagrāma, with markings like those of the ammonite, are worshipped by the principal sects of Vaishṇavas, as representing Vishṇu; also white agates as typifying Śiva, and red stones as symbolizing Gaṇeśa. Certain coral-like formations have also their religious value, and are revered as significant of particular attributes of the deity. The Māhātmya or divine glory of these stones is celebrated in the Padma-purāṇa.

We pass on now to sacred places. A Hindū's craving for some holy place of pilgrimage (*tīrtha*), to which he may hope to resort for a special blessing more than once in a lifetime, is not satisfied by a single Jerusalem, or a single Mecca.

India is studded with an increasing number of sacred places, from the very soil of which are supposed to exhale sanctity, salvation, and beatitude for the benefit of thousands of pilgrims who annually visit them. Pilgrimages to such spots (*tīrtha-yātrā*) are generally performed as acts of faith and devotion for the accumulation of religious merit, or to atone for sins.[1] Sometimes, however, they are undertaken for

[1] The pilgrims are often branded on their arms with a mark (*chāp*) of the *śankha*, *gadā*, *cakra*, *padma*, *kirīta* or *dhanus*, to

the performance of Śrāddha ceremonies in honour of departed ancestors, or for the recovery of some sick person,[1] or to convey the burnt remains of the bodies of deceased relations to some sacred shrine near a river, the object being to scatter the ashes on the purifying waters.

The multiplication of places of pilgrimage proceeded very rapidly. Rivers, as sources of fertility and purification, were at an early date invested with a sacred character. Every great river was supposed to be permeated with the divine essence, and its waters held to cleanse from all moral guilt and contamination. And as the Ganges was the most majestic, so it soon became the holiest and most revered of all rivers. No sin too heinous to be removed, no character too black to be washed clean by its waters. Hence the countless temples with flights of steps lining its banks; hence the array of priests called 'Sons of the Ganges,' sitting on the edge of its streams, ready to aid the ablutions of conscience-stricken bathers, and stamp them as white-washed when they emerge from its waters. Hence also the constant traffic carried on in transporting Ganges water in small bottles to all parts of the country.

The confluence of the Ganges with the Jumnā

---

serve as an evidence of their having accomplished a particular pilgrimage. At Dvārakā nearly 5,000 persons are annually branded.

[1] Colonel Sleeman records the case of a family of four persons who walked about fourteen hundred miles with a sick boy, carrying with them bottles of Ganges water to bathe the idol of Jagannāth in Orissa. The change of air cured the child, but the family of course attributed the cure to the gratitude of the idol.

(Yamunā) and Sarasvatī (supposed to flow underground) at Allahābād (Prayāga) is one of the most hallowed spots in all India. These three sacred streams form a sort of Tri-mūrti, or trinity of rivers, often personified as goddesses, and called Mothers. Then other rivers, such as the *Godāvarī* (also called Godā and Vṛiddha-gangā), *Narbadā* (properly Narmadā, also called Revā), *Taptī* (properly Tapatī, also called Tāpī), *Sābarmatī* (properly Sābhramatī), *Kistna* (properly Kṛishṇā), *Veṇā*, *Sarayu*, *Tunga-bhadrā*, and *Kāverī*, became rivals of this original sacred triad. Chapters, called Māhātmyas, extolling the virtue of their waters, and describing their consecration by gods and sages, were inserted in the Purāṇas. Thus, the sacredness of the Godāvarī is said to have been revealed by Rāma (to the Ṛishi Gotama), and that of the Sābarmatī by Kaśyapa.

And here we may note that the whole length of the banks of all the chief rivers of India, from their source to the sea, is regarded as holy ground. To follow their course on foot is considered a highly meritorious act. A pilgrim, for example, sets out from the source of the Ganges, at Gangotrī, and walks by the left bank of the river to its mouth, at Gangā-sāgara; then, turning round, he proceeds by the right side back to Gangotrī, whence he departed. This is called Pradakshiṇā, or Parikrama of the river, and takes six years to accomplish. In the same way a pilgrim starts from the source of the Narbadā, at Amara-kaṇṭak,—a peak of the Vindhya chain in Goṇḍwana,—and walks to the mouth, near Broach, and back. This takes three years. The rivers Godāvarī and Kṛishṇā require only two years for the same process. Of course, the merit accumulated is in proportion to the time occupied in the pilgrimage and the sacredness of the ground traversed.

But if rivers were believed to be pervaded by divinity, and their waters held capable of purging from all sin, it will not be matter of wonder that holy cities, towns, and bathing-places (*tīrthas*) rapidly arose on their banks. It was not difficult to stamp such places with a sacred character. One or other of the gods was described as connecting himself with particular localities. Thus, the sanctity of Benares, on the Ganges, was supposed to have been communicated by the god Śiva to his son Skanda (as recorded in the Kāśī-khaṇḍa of the Skanda-purāṇa), and the whole town therefore became sacred to the special worship of Śiva, who is alleged to have gone through severe austerities in the neighbourhood.

This celebrated city of Benares, which has a population of about 200,000, out of which at least 25,000 are Brāhmans, was probably one of the first to acquire a fame for sanctity, and it has always maintained its reputation as the most sacred spot in all India. Here, in this fortress of Hindūism, Brāhmanism displays itself in all its plenitude and power. Here the degrading effect of idolatry is visibly demonstrated as it is nowhere else except in the extreme south of India. Here temples, idols, and symbols, sacred wells, springs, and pools, are multiplied beyond all calculation. Here every particle of ground is believed to be hallowed, and the very air holy. The number of temples is at least two thousand, not counting innumerable smaller shrines. In the principal temple of Śiva, called Viśveśvara, are collected in one spot several thousand idols and symbols, the whole number scattered throughout the city being, it is thought, at least half a million.

Benares, indeed, must always be regarded as the Hindū's Jerusalem. The desire of a pious man's life is to accomplish at least one pilgrimage to what he regards as a portion of heaven let down upon earth ; and if he can die within the holy circuit of the Pančakośī, stretching with a radius of ten miles around the city,—nay, if any human being die there, be he Asiatic or European,—no previously-incurred guilt, however heinous, can prevent his attainment of celestial bliss.

For a long time the river Ganges and the city Benares occupied a position far above all other rivers and all other sacred cities ; but as the Āryans spread themselves from the north-west, eastward, westward, and southward, the Brāhmans who settled down in other places naturally became jealous of the monopoly enjoyed by those in Benares. If any natural phenomenon—a volcanic crater, a fissure in the soil, a hot spring, a cavern or rock of peculiar shape—existed anywhere, it was pressed into the service, and made to subserve the purposes of the priests. A kind of free trade in the invention of myths for the consecration of particular spots was thus introduced. For instance, in Kāttiwār there is a spring, the water of which is said to have been formed from the perspiration of Kṛishṇa's body. So also many legends were connected with the great idol Jagan-nāth at Purī, in Orissa, which is said to contain Kṛishṇa's bones.

New Māhātmyas were then composed and inserted in some of the Purāṇas (often in the Skanda), making a god or holy sage reveal and extol the praises of a particular spot intended to be elevated to a high position among the consecrated places of India.

Place after place was declared consecrated ground. Prayāga at Allahābād and Gayā probably achieved a reputation for sanctity soon after Benares. Preachers were sent all over India to recite the Māhātmyas of innumerable rival localities.

To this day the priests of Benares, Gayā, Allahābād, and other sacred places send agents to every town and large railway station in India, who are commissioned to persuade pilgrims to visit their own shrines. When once a stream of pilgrims sets in a particular direction, it very soon gathers strength. One devotee follows another, and in this manner the fame of many new places is established. Paṇḍharpur, in the Dekhan, which contains a shrine of Kṛishṇa called Viṭhobā (celebrated by the Marāṭhī poet Tukārām), is a city which has in this way risen quite recently to importance.

At nearly every sacred place the number of shrines to be visited and of ceremonies to be performed occupies many days, and no pilgrim can go through all the duties required of him without the aid of the Brāhmans attached to the locality, who exact fees even from the poorest, and receive large sums of money from rich persons. At some sacred places religious gatherings occur every year, at others after certain intervals. The fullest often take place once in twelve years, when the planet Jupiter enters a particular sign,[1] on which occasion the concourse of

[1] For example, at Haridwār, when Jupiter enters the sign

people is so enormous that loss of life sometimes happens from overcrowding. Many think to enhance the merit of their pilgrimages by imposing on themselves the most toilsome tasks on the road; such, for example, as advancing towards their destination by continued prostrations of the body, or, as it is termed, 'measuring their lengths' for hundreds of miles.

In some ancient texts only seven principal holy towns are enumerated; viz.:—

Kāśī or Benares; *Mathurā* or Muttra, the capital of Kansa, conquered by Kṛishṇa, on the Jumnā, near Agra; *Haridwār* (or Māyā), where the Ganges, descending from the Himālayas, first enters the plains; *Ayodhyā* (now Fyzabad), the ancient capital of Rāma-candra, near Lucknow; *Dvārakā*, the city of Kṛishṇa, in Gujarāt; *Avantikā* or Oujein; and *Kāncī* or Conjevaram (i.e. *Kāncī-puram*), near Madras.[1]

Again, in others, the chief sacred cities are declared to be only three—*Benares*, resorted to for self-mortification; *Prayāga* (Allahābād) for religious shaving; and *Gayā* for *S'rāddha* ceremonies. At the last place a footprint of Vishṇu is the great object of adoration.

Seven Sangamas, or river confluences—all called Prayāgas—are pronounced especially sacred:—

That of the Ganges and Jumnā, called Bhaṭṭa-prayāga; of the Leti and Alaka-nandā, called Vishṇu-prayāga; of the

---

Aquarius (*Kumbha*), at Prayāga when he enters *Makara*, and at Tryambak when he enters Leo (*Sinha*).

[1] There are said to be two Kāncīs, one called Vishṇu-kāncī, and the other S'iva-kāncī. They are merely the two great temples at either end of Conjevaram = Kāncī-puram.

Alaka-nandā and Nandā, called Nandā-prayāga; of the Piṇḍār and Alaka-nandā, called Karṇa-prayāga; of the Mandākinī and Alaka-nandā, called Rudra-prayāga; of the Bhāgīrathī and Mandākinī, called Deva-prayāga; of the Kṛishṇā and Veṇā, called Dakshiṇa-prayāga (in the Dekhan).

The sources, and sometimes the mouths, of these and other rivers are always esteemed places of pilgrimage; for example:—

Gangotrī, the source of the Ganges; *Jumnotrī*, of the Jumnā; *Amara-kaṇṭak*, in the Vindhya, of the Narbadā; *Mahābaleśvar*, of the Kṛishṇā and Veṇā (Kistna); *Tāpī-mūla*, of the Taptī, in Berār; *Gangā-sāgara*, the mouth of the Ganges.

Then there are four specially holy Dhāmas or residence of deities, viz.:—

Jagan-nāth, at Purī, in Orissa; *Dvārakā*[1] (also one of the seven holy towns before named); *Badarī-kedāra* or *Badarī-nāth*, in the Himālayas (one of the sources of the Ganges); *Rāmeśvara*, on an island six miles from land, between India and Ceylon.

And twelve sacred places containing celebrated Lingas of Śiva, viz.:—

Somnāth, in Kāttiwār; *Mallikārjuna*, on the 'Srī-śaila mountain, in the Karnatic; *Mahākāla* or *Mahākāleśvara*, in Ujjayinī (Oujein), to the north of Indore; *Oṃ-kāra*, on an island in the river Narbadā; *Kedāra* or *Kedāreśvara*, in the Himālayas; *Bhīma-śankara*, at the source of the river Bhīmā, near Pūnah; *Viśvanāth*, in Benares; *Tryambaka-nāth*, near Nāsik, on the Godāvarī; *Vaidya-nāth* (or Vaijanāth), about 100 miles from Ahmednagar; *Nāganāth*, or *Nāgeśvara*, beyond Ahmed-

---

[1] There are two Dvārakās at the distance of fourteen miles from each other; one is called Gomatī Dvārakā, and the other, Beyt. When the idol was removed from the former to Dakore, a new one was placed in Gomatī by S'ankarāčārya, who has a monastery there, while Vallabhāčārya gave an idol to Beyt.

nagar in the Nizām's dominions; *Rāmanāth* or *Rāmeśvara*, near Adam's Bridge, between India and Ceylon; *Ghṛishṇeś-vara*, at Ellora, near Aurungabad.

Five divine lakes (*Sarovara*), or holy tanks, are also enumerated; viz.:—

Nārāyaṇa, in Kutch; *Pushkara*, in Ājmīr; *Bindu*, in Sidh-pur, about 60 miles from Ahmedabad; *Pampā*, in the Kar-natic, and *Mānasa* (commonly called Māna-sarovar), in the Himālaya mountains.

There are also four celebrated shrines of god-desses:—

Mahā-lakshmī, at Kolapur; *Bhavānī*, near Sholapur; *Reṇukā*, at Mātāpura; *Yogeśvarī*, about 80 miles from Ah mednagar.

And four monasteries of Śankarācārya, one at each extremity of India, viz.:—

S'āradā-maṭha, at Gomatī Dvārakā; *S'ṛingerī-maṭha*, in the Karnatic, near Mysore; *Jyotir-maṭha*, near Badarī-nāth, one of the sources of the Ganges; and *Vardhana-maṭha*, at Purī.

A few other well-known sacred places are:—

C'itra-kote, near Allahābād, the first abode of Rāma and Lakshmaṇa after their exile from Ayodhyā; *Prabhāsa*, near Somnāth and Dvārakā, where Kṛishṇa's kinsmen, the Yādavas, destroyed themselves; *S'rī-nāth* or *Nāth-dvār*, near Udaipur (the temple of which has an idol from Govardhana); *Amara-nāth*, in Kāśmīr; *Jvālā-mukhī*, a small volcanic crater near Amritsar, in the Panjab; *Dākore*, in Gujarāt, celebrated for the idol of Kṛishṇa (called Raṇ-chor) brought from Dvārakā.

Nāsik, on the Godāvarī, where Lakshmaṇa cut off the nose of the demon S'ūrpa-ṇakhā; *Kuru-kshetra*, near Delhi, where the great battles of the Mahābhārata were fought; *Rāja-ṭur*, near C'itra-kote, the residence of Tulsī-dās; *Gāḍhadā*, in Kātti-wār, where the body of Svāmi-Nārāyaṇa (see p. 145) was burnt; *Pālitāna* (or *S'atrunjaya*), a sacred hill of the Jains in Kāṭiwār; *Amritsar*, in the Panjāb, the sacred city of the Sikhs.

It appears, then, that almost the whole circle of the sciences—zoology, botany, mineralogy, and geography—is in India taken into the service of religious superstition. Even astronomy and chronology are utilized in the same way. If a full moon fall on a Monday, this is an astronomical coincidence that must be by all means turned to the best account. It is a moment particularly favourable for charitable acts; and a gift of one rupee at such a time is equal to one thousand at any other.

The Nakshatras—twenty-seven constellations which in Indian astronomy separate the moon's path into twenty-seven divisions, as the signs of the Zodiac do that of the sun into twelve—are regarded as deities who exert a vast influence on the destiny of men, not only at the moment of their entrance into the world, but during their whole passage through it. These formidable constellations are consulted at births, marriages, and on all occasions of family rejoicing, distress, or calamity. No one undertakes a journey or any important matter except on days which the aspect of the Nakshatras renders lucky and auspicious. If any constellation is unfavourable, it must by all means be propitiated by a ceremony called *S'ānti.*

Much the same may be said of the supposed influence of the nine Grahas (see p. 166), all regarded as planets. Similarly it is held that mysterious attributes and properties attach to every month of the year and every day of the month. The Māhātmyas, or religious excellence and value of months, such as Śrāvaṇa, Vaiśākha, and especially of the intercalary month (called *Adhika-māsa*, *Mala-māsa*, *Purushottama-māsa*), have all been written and inserted in the Purāṇas. When the intercalary month comes round every third year, numerous preachers make the most of their opportunity, and read its Māhātmya in the streets of large towns, hoping thereby to stimulate the generosity of the people, and extract large charitable gifts. Certain sacred days at the changes of the moon are called 'Parvans,' and a glance at the Hindū calendar is sufficient to show that no nation upon earth rejoices in a longer list of holidays and festivals (*utsava*), qualified by fasts (*upavāsā*), vigils (*jāgaraṇa*) and seasons of mortification. Most of these festivals and fasts are fixed for certain Tithis or lunar days, each lunation or period of rather more than twenty-seven days being divided into thirty Tithis, fifteen of which during the moon's increase constitute the light half of the month, and the other fifteen the dark half. Some festivals, however, are regulated by the supposed motions of the sun. The festivals and fasts most commonly observed throughout the year may be enumerated as follows :—

1. *Makara-sankrānti*, or the commencement of the sun's northern course in the heavens. On this day, the first of the solar month Māgha (about the beginning of January), the sun having reached the most southern point of the ecliptic (according to the Hindū reckoning), begins his northern course (*uttarāyaṇa*), which he continues till the end of June. It is a period of great rejoicing everywhere, and especially

at Prayāga (Allahābād), the confluence of the Jumnā and Ganges, where a celebrated Melā (religious fair) takes place. In the South of India this festival is commonly called 'Pongal,' and is the commencement of the Tamil year. Cattle are decorated with garlands, led about in procession, treated with especial veneration and exempted from labour.

2. *S'rī-pan̒camī*, on the 5th of the light half of Māgha (January-February), in honour of Sarasvatī (called Śrī), goddess of arts and learning. Implements of writing and books are therefore worshipped (see pp. 90, 91).

3. *S'iva-rātri*, in honour of Śiva, held on the 14th of the dark half of Māgha (about the middle or end of February). A strict fast is observed during the day, and a vigil held at night, when the Linga is worshipped. At this season many pilgrims flock to the places dedicated to Śiva.

4. *Holī*, now generally identified with the *Dola-yātrā* or swinging festival, celebrated as a kind of Hindū Saturnalia or Carnival, and very popular all over India. It commences about ten days before the full moon of Phālguna (February-March), but is usually only observed for the last three or four days, terminating with the full moon. During this festival boys dance about in the streets, and the inhabitants of the houses sprinkle the passers-by with red or yellow powder, or play practical jokes. Towards the close of the festival a bonfire is lighted and games (representing the frolics of the young Kṛishṇa) take place round the expiring embers.

5. *Rāma-navamī*, the birthday of Rāma-c̒andra, on the 9th of the light half of the month C'aitra (March-

April), kept by some as a strict fast. The temples of Rāma are illuminated, and the image of Rāma adorned with costly ornaments. The Rāmāyaṇa is read in the temples, and Nautches are kept up during the night.

6. *Nāga-pañcamī*, a festival in honour of the Nāgas (see p. 169), on the 5th day of the light half of Śrāvaṇa.

7. *Kṛishṇa janmāshṭamī*, the birthday of Kṛishṇa, on the 8th of the dark half of the month Bhādra, and in the south of Śrāvaṇa (July-August), one of the greatest of all Hindū holidays. The months of the Northern and Southern Brāhmans differ in Krishṇa-paksha.

8. *Gaṇeśa-caturthī*, the birthday of Gaṇeśa, on the 4th of the light half of the month Bhādra (August-September). Clay figures of the deity are made, and after being worshipped for two days, or in some cases ten days, are thrown into water.

9. *Durgā-pūjā*, or *Nava-rātri*, commencing on the 1st, and ending on the 10th day of the light half of Āśvina (September-October). This festival, celebrated in Bengal and other parts of India, is supposed to be connected with the autumnal equinox. It is held in commemoration of the victory of Durgā, wife of Śiva, over a buffalo-headed demon (*Mahishāsur*). Her image is worshipped for nine days, and then cast into the water. The tenth day is called *Vijaya-daśamī*, or *Daśa-harā.*

10. *Rama-līlā.*—On the day when the Bengālis assign their images of Durgā to the waters, the Hindūs of other provinces celebrate the Rāma-līlā, a dramatic representation of the carrying off of Sītā,

concluding with the death of Rāvaṇa (see p. 111), of which the 9th day of the Durgā-pūjā is the anniversary.

11. *Dīpālī* or *Dīvālī* (properly *Dīpāvalī*), 'the feast of lamps,' on the last two days of the dark half of Āśvina (September-October), and the new moon and four following days of Kārttika, in honour of Vishṇu's wife Lakshmī, and of Śiva's wife Bhavānī (Pārvatī).

12. *Kārttika-pūrṇimā*, the full moon of the month Kārttika (October-November), a festival kept in honour of Śiva's victory over the demon Tripurāsura.

We must now bring our account of Hindūism to a close. We cannot hope to have succeeded in unravelling all the knots of an intricate subject. Sufficient at least has been written to show that the Hindūs are a profoundly religious people. A religion of some kind they must have—a religion which will stir the depths of the heart, and give room for the exercise of faith and love.

The ancient fortress of Hindūism, with its four sides, Monotheism, Pantheism, Dualism, and Polytheism, is everywhere tottering and ready to fall. Let not Christianity undervalue its obligations to education, which has, so to speak, served as a mighty lever for upheaving the massive fabric of the Hindū system. But the education we are giving in India has little effect on the heart, and has certainly no power to regenerate it. What then is to become of the masses of the people when their ancient faith sinks from beneath their feet? Only two other homes are before them—a cold theism and a heart-stirring Christianity. They are both already established in the soil of India. But Christianity is spreading its boundaries more widely, and striking its foundations more deeply. It appeals directly to the heart. It is exactly suited to the needs of the masses of the people of India. In Christianity alone is their true home.

But much has still to be done to convince them of this. Of course, too much stress can scarcely be laid on the degrading tendencies of idolatry. Yet there are three points which ought to be still more forcibly insisted on by our missionaries as distinguishing Christianity from all other systems; first, the co-ordination and union of the human and divine, of man's work and God's work, as exhibited, for example, in our Sacred Scriptures; secondly, the everlasting permanence and even intensification of the personality of man as distinct from the personality of God; thirdly, the perfect personality of God as revealed in Christ. As to the third point, it should be made quite clear that Muhammadans, Hindūs, Buddhists, and Jains have nothing parallel to the great truth of the perfect personality of the God-man Christ.

Let the proselyting Muslim proudly declare, when confronted with the opponents of his own creed in the bazaars of India, that he will meet his foe with no other weapon than the sword of the Kurān. Let the Hindū philosopher calmly intrench himself behind the Pantheism of his Veda, and the theistical Brāhma behind the strength of his dogma that 'God is one,' while the infidel Jain looks down with serene apathy from the heights of his atheism on a struggle to which he is indifferent. Then let the Christian missionary, without despising the formidable Goliaths to which he is opposed, but with the quiet confidence of a David in the strength of his own weapons, go forth fearlessly with the simple sling and stone of the Gospel in his hand and do battle with his enemies, not forgetting to use the Sword of the Spirit with its nine irresistible thrusts—love, joy, peace, long-suffering, gentleness, goodness, faith, meekness, temperance.

Much ground, indeed, has been already won by the soldiers of the Cross; but to secure a more hopeful advance of Christianity throughout India, a large accession to the missionary ranks of well-trained men, thoroughly conversant with the systems against which they have to contend, and prepared to *live* as well as preach the simple story of the Gospel of Christ, is urgently needed. And far more than this is needed for the complete triumph of God's truth in India. Nothing less is demanded of us Englishmen, to whose charge the Almighty has committed the souls and bodies of two hundred and forty millions of His creatures, than that every man among us, whether clerical or lay, should strive to be a missionary according to the standard set up by the first great Missionary—Christ Himself. Let no lower standard of our duty satisfy us. So will the good time arrive when not only every ear shall have heard the good news of the reconciliation of man to his Maker, but every tongue also of every native of India—from Cape Comorin to the Himālaya mountains—shall confess that Jesus Christ is Lord, to the glory of God the Father.

APPENDIX.

DISTINCTIVE FEATURES OF THE SIX SCHOOLS OF PHILOSOPHY.

THE names of the Six Schools of Philosophy have been already given, and the doctrines common to them all briefly explained (see p. 46). No student of Hindūism, however, and certainly no missionary, ought to be satisfied without acquiring a clear and accurate knowledge of the principal distinguishing characteristics of the six philosophical schools. The more advanced scholar will, of course, do well to study the original Sūtras in which the dogmas of each school are enunciated. But a concise outline of each system may be found useful by those who have not time to make themselves Sanskritists.

In endeavouring to give a trustworthy sketch of this difficult and intricate subject, it will be convenient to begin with the Nyāya of Gotama, with its supplement, the Vaiśeshika, not because the Nyāya is first in order of time, but because it is generally first studied, and much of its terminology is adopted by the other systems.

The Nyāya proper.

The word Nyāya signifies 'going into a subject,' *i.e.* investigating it analytically. In this sense of 'analysis,' the word *Nyāya* is exactly opposed to *Sankhyā*, 'synthesis.' It is common to suppose that the Nyāya is chiefly concerned with logic, but this is merely one part of a single topic, the fact rather being that this system was intended to furnish a correct method of philosophical inquiry into *all the objects and subjects* of human knowledge, including, *amongst others*, the process of reasoning and laws of thought.

The Nyāya proper propounds in its first Sūtra sixteen topics, the first of which is *Pramāṇa*, *i. e.* the means or instrument by which Pramā, or the right measure of a subject, is to be obtained. The different processes by which the mind arrives at true and accurate knowledge are four; viz.—*a*. *Pratyaksha*, 'perception by the senses'; *b*. *Anumāna*, 'inference'; *c*. *Upamāna*, 'comparison'; *d*. *S'abda*, 'verbal authority,' or 'trustworthy testimony,' including Vedic revelation.

The treatment of the second of these four, 'inference,' indicates that the Hindūs have not, like other nations, borrowed their logic from the Greeks. It is divided into five Avayavas or 'members.' 1. The *pratijnā*, or proposition (stated hypothetically). 2. The *hetu*, or reason. 3. The *udāharaṇa*, or example (= major premiss). 4. The *upanaya*, or application of the reason (= minor premiss). 5. The *nigamana*, or conclusion, *i. e.* the proposition re-stated as proved. This method of splitting an argument into five divisions is thus illustrated: 1. The hill is fiery; 2. for it smokes; 3. whatever smokes is fiery, as a kitchen-hearth; 4. this hill smokes; 5. therefore this hill is fiery.

Here we have a combination of enthymeme and syllogism, which seems clumsy by the side of Aristotle's conciser method; but it possesses some advantages when regarded not as a syllogism, but as a full and complete rhetorical statement of an argument.

Perhaps the most noticeable peculiarity in the Indian method, stamping it as an original and independent analysis of the laws of thought, is the use of the curious terms *Vyāpti*, 'pervasion'; *Vyāpaka*, 'pervader'; and *Vyāpya*, 'to be pervaded.' These terms are employed in making a universal affirmation, or in affirming universal distribution; as, for example, 'Wherever there is smoke there is fire.' In such a case an Indian logician always expresses himself by saying that there is an invariably pervading concomitance of fire with smoke. Fire is therefore called the pervader, and smoke the pervaded; and the argument would be thus briefly stated by a *Naiyāyika*: 'The mountain has invariably fire-pervaded smoke, therefore it has fire.'

The second topic of the Nyāya proper is *Prameya*, *i.e.* the subjects of *Pramā*, or the subjects about which right knowledge is to be obtained. These are twelve: viz. 1. Soul (*ātman*). 2. Body (*śarīra*). 3. Senses (*indriya*). 4. Objects of sense (*artha*). 5. Understanding or intellection (*buddhi*). 6. Mind (*manas*). 7. Activity (*pravṛitti*). 8. Faults (*dosha*). 9. Transmigration (*pretya-bhāva*). 10. Consequences or fruits (*phala*). 11. Pain (*duḥkha*). 12. Emancipation (*apavarga*).

With regard to the fourteen other topics, they seem to be not so much philosophical categories as an enumeration of the regular stages through which a controversy is likely to pass. In India argument slides into wrangling disputation even more easily than in Europe, and the remaining topics certainly illustrate very curiously the captious propensities of a Hindū disputant, leading him to be quick in repartee, and ready with specious objections to the most conclusive argument.

There is, first, the state of *Saṃśaya*, or 'doubt about the point to be discussed.' Next, the *Prayojana*, or 'motive for discussing it.' Next follows a *Dṛishṭānta*, or 'example' leading to the *Siddhānta*, or 'established conclusion.' Then comes an objector with his *Avayava*, or 'argument split up,' as we have seen, into five members. Next follows the *Tarka* or 'refutation (*reductio ad absurdum*) of his objection,' and the *Nirṇaya*, or 'ascertainment of the true state of the case.' But this is not enough to satisfy a Hindū's passion for disputation. Every side of a question must be examined—every possible objection stated—and so a further *Vāda*, or 'controversy,' takes place, which of course leads to *Jalpa*, 'mere wrangling,' followed by *Vitaṇḍa*, 'cavilling'; *Hetv-ābhāsa*, 'fallacious reasoning'; *C'hala*, 'quibbling artifices'; *Jāti*, 'futile replies'; and *Nigraha-sthāna*, 'the putting an end to all discussion,' by a demonstration of the objector's incapacity for argument.

After enumerating these sixteen topics, Gotama proceeds to show how false notions are at the root of all misery. For from false notions comes the fault of liking, disliking, or being indifferent to anything; from that fault proceeds activity; from this mistaken activity proceed actions involving either merit or demerit, which merit or demerit forces a man to pass through repeated births for the sake of its reward or punishment. From these births proceeds misery, and it is the aim of philosophy to correct the false notions at the root of this misery.

2 *The Vaiśeshika* (supplement of the Nyāya).

The Vaiśeshika may be called a supplement of the Nyāya proper. It is attributed to a sage named Kaṇāda ('atom-eater'), and is not so much a branch of the Nyāya as a development of it, extending the system to physical investigations, which it conducts very imperfectly, it is true, and often with strange fancies and absurd blunders, but, nevertheless, with occasional exactness, and not unfrequently with singular sagacity. It is, perhaps, the most interesting of all the systems, both from its more practical character and from the parallels it offers to European philosophical ideas. It begins by arranging its inquiries under seven *Padārthas*, or categories (*i. e.* enumeration of certain general properties or attributes that may be predicated of existing things), which, as they are more properly categories than the topics of tne Nyāya proper, are now the generally-received categories of the Naiyāyikas. They are as follows:—1. Substance (*dravya*); 2. Quality or property (*guṇa*); 3. Act or action (*karman*); 4. Generality or community of properties (*sāmānya*); 5. Particularity or individuality (*viśesha*); 6. Coinherence or perpetual intimate relation (*samavāya*); 7. Non-existence, or negation of existence (*abhāva*).

Kaṇāda, however, enumerated only six categories: the seventh was added by later writers.

The seven categories have most of them subdivisions. Those of the first category, *Dravya*, substance, are nine, to wit—earth, water, light, air, ether, time, space, soul, and the internal organ or mind.

The first four of these nine, and the last (viz. *Manas*, 'the mind'), are held to be atomic, and the first four are both eternal and non-eternal; non-eternal in their various compounds, eternal in their ultimate atoms to which they must be traced back.

As to the second category, *Guṇa*, 'quality,' there are seventeen qualities inherent in the nine substances; viz. colour, savour, odour, tangibility, numbers, extensions, individuality, conjunction, disjunction, priority, posteriority, intellections, pleasure, pain, desire, aversion, volitions. Seven others are said to be implied; viz. gravity, fluidity, viscidity, self-reproduction, merit, demerit, and sound; making twenty-four in all.

Sixteen of these qualities belong to material substances. The other eight—viz. intellection, volition, desire, aversion, pleasure, pain, merit, and demerit—are the properties of the soul.

The third category, *Karman*, 'act,' consists of five kinds of acts; viz. elevation, depression, contraction, dilatation, and motion; and the fourth, *Sāmānya*, generality of properties, is said to be twofold; viz. higher and lower generality, to wit, that of genus and of species.

The fifth category, *Viśesha*, 'particularity,' belongs

to the nine eternal substances of the first category, all of which have an eternal ultimate difference, distinguishing each from the other. Hence the system is called Vaiśeshika.

The sixth category, *Samavāya*, 'coinherence,' is of only one kind. It is the coinherence between a substance and its qualities, between atoms and what is formed out of them, between a genus or species and its individuals, between any object and the general idea connected with it, and is thought to be a real entity.

As to the seventh, *Abhāva*, 'non-existence,' four kinds are specified; viz. antecedent non-existence, cessation of existence, mutual non-existence (as of a jar in cloth), absolute non-existence.

In the Vaiśeshika system the formation of the world is supposed to be effected by the aggregation of atoms. These are innumerable and eternal, and are eternally aggregated, disintegrated, and redisintegrated by the power of Adṛishṭa (see p. 51). An atom is defined as 'something existing, having no cause, and eternal.' It is, moreover, described as less than the least, invisible, intangible, indivisible, imperceptible by the senses; and each atom has a *Viśesha*, or eternal essence of its own. The combination of these atoms is first into an aggregate of two. Three of them, again, are supposed to combine into a particle, called *Trasareṇu*, which, like a mote in a sunbeam, has just sufficient magnitude to be perceptible.

With regard to a Supreme Being, the name of *Īśvara*, 'Supreme Lord,' is introduced once into Gotama's Sūtras, but is not found in Kaṇāda's.

Probably the belief of both was that the formation of the world was simply the result of *Adṛishṭa*, 'the unseen force,' derived from the works or acts of a previous world. This force becomes in Hindū philosophy a kind of god, if not the only god. Later Naiyāyika writers, however, affirm the existence of a Supreme Soul (*paramātman*), distinct from the living human Soul (*jīvātman*); and this Supreme Soul is described by them as eternal, immutable, omniscient, without form, all-pervading, all-powerful, and moreover as the framer of the universe.

Again, they hold the living individual souls of men (*jīvātman*) to be eternal, manifold, eternally separate from each other, and distinct from the body, senses, and mind, yet capable of apprehension, volition, desire, aversion, pleasure, pain, merit, and demerit.; and they hold them to be infinite, ubiquitous, and *diffused everywhere throughout space*, so that a man's soul is as much in England as in Calcutta, though it can only apprehend and feel and act where the body happens to be.

The Nyāya idea of the mind (*manas*), which it calls an internal organ, is that it is like the soul, a Dravya, or eternal substance. Instead, however, of being diffused everywhere like the soul, it is atomic, like earth, water, fire, and air. In fact, it can only admit one thought at a time. If it were infinite like the soul, all apprehensions and conceptions might be contemporaneous, which is impossible.

It is clear then that the Vaiśeshika cosmogony is dualistic in the sense of assuming the existence of *eternal atoms*, side by side either with *eternal souls*, or with the Supreme Soul of the universe. It is opposed to any theory which would make an impure and evil world spring from a pure and perfect spirit. Nor does it undertake to decide positively what it cannot prove dialectically—the precise relation between soul and matter.

3. *The Sānkhya.*

The Sānkhya philosophy, founded by a sage named *Kapila*, though probably prior in date, is generally studied next to the Nyāya, and is more categorically dualistic. It wholly repudiates the notion that impure matter can originate from pure spirit, and, of course, denies that anything can be produced out of nothing.

The following aphorisms propound its doctrine of evolution :—

"There cannot be production of something out of nothing ; that which is not cannot be developed into that which is. The production of what does not already exist (potentially) is impossible, like a horn on a man ; because there must of necessity be a material out of which a product is developed, and because everything cannot occur everywhere at all times, and because anything possible must be produced from something competent to produce it."

In the Sānkhya, therefore, instead of an analytical inquiry into the universe as actually existing, arranged under topics and categories, we have a synthetical system starting from an original primordial *Tattva* or 'eternally existing essence,' called *Prakṛiti*, 'that which evolves, or produces, or brings forth (*prakaroti*) everything else,' and described in the following aphorisms :—

"From the absence of a root in the root, the root of all things is rootless."

"Even if there be a succession of causes (one before the other), there must be a halt at some one point ; and so Prakṛiti is only a name for the primal source (of all productions)."

It should be noted, at the outset, that Prakṛiti, though a subtle elementary essence, is yet itself supposed to be made up of three constituent principles or elementary substances in equipoise, called Guṇas, (from the word *guṇa*, a cord, because they bind the soul with a triple bond), viz. goodness or purity (*sattva*), passion or activity (*rajas*), and darkness or stolidity (*tamas*). These three Sānkhyan Guṇas are constantly referred to in Indian literature, and it is most important that the student of Hindūism should endeavour to understand the ideas they convey. They are by no means to be confounded with the Nyāya Guṇas (see p. 191). They are the actual substances or ingredients of which Prakṛiti is constituted, just as trees are of a forest. Moreover, they are supposed to make up the whole world of sense evolved out of Prakṛiti, although in this case they are not conjoined in equal quantities, but in varying proportions, one or other being in excess.[1] In the case of a man, they make him divine and noble, thoroughly human and selfish, or bestial and ignorant, according to the predominance of goodness, passion, or darkness respectively.

This remarkable doctrine of three eternal principles, *Sattva*, *Rajas*, and *Tamas*, may be called the Sānkhyan trinity, just as the idea of *Saċ-ċid-ānanda* (see p. 52) may be regarded as the trinity of the Vedāntist.

Beginning, then, from the original eternal rootless germ *Prakṛiti*,[2] (also called *Pradhāna*, chief one; *Avyakta*, unevolved; *Māyā*, power of illusion), the Sānkhya counts up (*san-khyāti*) synthetically (whence its name of 'synthetic enumeration') twenty-three other Tattvas or entities,—all productions of the first, and evolving themselves spontaneously out of it, as cream out of milk, or milk out of a cow,—while it carefully distinguishes them all from a twenty-fifth, *Purusha*, the soul, which is wholly in its own nature destitute of Guṇas, though liable to be bound by the Guṇas of Prakṛiti.

The process is thus stated in the Sānkhya-kārikā:

> "The root and substance of all things (except soul) is Prakṛiti. It is no production. Seven things produced by it are also producers. Thence come sixteen productions (*vikāra*). Soul, the twenty-fifth essence, is neither a production nor producer."

---

[1] It cannot be too often repeated, that they are not to be confounded with the Nyāya Guṇas. In fact, they are evidently rather substances or principles than qualities, though *guṇa* also means 'quality'; and although such expressions as goodness, purity, &c., convey more the notion of a quality than of a substance. May not the whole idea have been suggested by the three forms of matter? At any rate, even modern chemists acknowledge a kind of material triad of substances,—solid, liquid, and gaseous.

[2] The translation *Nature*, often given for this word, is altogether misleading. Better equivalents would be such expressions as Evolvent, Evolver, Producer, Originator, &c.

The first production of the eternal Producer is *Buddhi* or 'intelligence,' also termed *Mahat*, from its being the *Great* source of the next producer, *Ahankāra*, and the eleventh organ, *Manas*). Third in order comes this *Ahankāra*, the 'I-maker,' *i. e.* self-consciousness, or the sense of individuality, which produces the next five principles, called *Tanmātras*, or 'subtle elementary particles.' These eight constitute the producers.

Then follow the sixteen that are productions (*Vikāra*) only. And first in order, as produced by the Tanmātras, come the five grosser elements (*mahābhūta*), as follows :—

1. *Ākāśa*, 'ether,' with the distinguishing property or substratum of sound (which is the *vishaya* or object for a corresponding organ of sense, the ear). 2. *Vāyu*, 'air,' with the property of tangibility (which is the *vishaya* for the skin). 3. *Tejas* or *Jyotis*, 'fire or light,' with the property of form or colour (which is the *vishaya* for the eye). 4. *Apas*, 'water,' with the property of taste (which is the *vishaya* for the tongue). 5. *Pṛithivī*, or *bhūmi*, 'earth,' with the property of odour or smell (which is the *vishaya* for the nose).

Each of these elements, after the first, has also the property of the preceding besides its own.

Next follow the eleven organs produced, like the Tanmātras, by the third producer, Ahan-kāra. These are the five organs of sense, the five organs of action,[1] and an eleventh organ standing between them, viz. *Manas*, 'the mind,' which is regarded as an internal organ of perception, volition, and action. The eight producers, then, with the five grosser elements and the eleven organs, constitute the true elements, and constituent substances of the phenomenal world. As, however, the most important of the producers, after

[1] The *buddhīndriyāṇi*, or organs of sense, are ear, skin, eye, nose, tongue; the *karmendriyāṇi*, organs of action, are larynx, hand, foot, excretory and generative organs.

the mere unintelligent original germ, is the third, called *Ahankāra*, 'self-consciousness,' the Sānkhya appears to maintain that the whole world of sense is practically created by the individual Ego, who is, nevertheless, quite distinct from the soul, as this soul is supposed to possess in itself no real consciousness of separate individuality, though deluded by it.[1]

But although Prakṛiti is the sole originator of creation, yet, according to the pure Sānkhya, it does not create for itself, but rather for each individual soul; nor indeed does it create at all to any practical purpose unless it comes into union with Purusha, like a crystal vase with a flower. Souls, indeed, exist eternally separate from each other, and from the Evolver Prakṛiti, and with whatever form of body they may be joined, they are held to be all intrinsically equal, and each retains its individuality, remaining one and unchanged through all transmigrations. But each separate soul is a witness of the act of a separate creation without participating in the act. It is a looker on, uniting itself with unintelligent *Prakṛiti*, as a lame man mounted on a blind man's shoulders, for the sake of observing the phenomena of creation, which Prakṛiti herself is unable to observe.

It appears, too, that all Prakṛiti's performances are solely for the benefit of soul, who receives her favours ungratefully. Indeed the object of the Sānkhya system is to effect the liberation of *Purusha* or soul from the fetters which bind it, in consequence of its union with Prakṛiti. This is done by conveying the *Pramā*, or correct knowledge of the twenty-four constituent principles of creation, and rightly discriminating the soul from them; its *Pramāṇas* (see p. 188),

[1] This idea of personal individual creation is what chiefly distinguishes the Sānkhya from the pantheism of the Vedānta, which denies all real personal individuality.

or 'means of obtaining the correct measure of existing things,' being reduced from four to three; viz., perception by the senses (*dṛishṭa*), inference (*anumāna*), and credible assertion or trustworthy testimony (*āpta-vaćana*).

No one can doubt that the Sānkhyan view of the soul is inferior to that of the Nyāya, which ascribes to it, when joined to mind, activity, volition, thought, and feeling. Obviously, too, the pure Sānkhya is more atheistical than the pure Nyāya; for if the Creation produced by the Evolver, *Prakṛiti*, has an existence of its own independent of all connection with the particular Purusha to which it is joined, there can be no need of an intelligent Creator of the world, or even of any superintending power.

Notwithstanding these atheistical tendencies, the charge of unorthodoxy is evaded by a confession of faith in the Veda. Some adherents of the Sānkhya maintain the existence of a supreme Soul, called *Hiraṇya-garbha*, and of a general ideal phenomenal universe with which that supreme Soul is connected, and into which all the subcreations of inferior souls are gathered.

It is remarkable that this singular theory of the relationship between spirit and matter, involving as it does a strange jumble of physical and metaphysical subtleties, has always had peculiar charms for the Hindū mind. Not that the uneducated masses could make anything of the mysticism of a primordial eternal germ evolving out of itself twenty-three substances to form a visible world for the soul, described as apathetic, inactive, devoid of all qualities, and a mere indifferent spectator; but that ordinary men are only too prone to accept any theory of the origin of the universe which makes the acts of the Creator harmonize with their own operations and the phenomena which surround them. Even the most illiterate

Hindū, therefore, was well able to understand and adopt the idea of a universe proceeding from Prakṛiti and Purusha as from father and mother. Indeed the idea of a union between the female principle, regarded as an energy or capacity (*śakti*), and the male principle, regarded as a generator, is, as we have already seen (see p. 123), of great antiquity in the Hindū system.

It is noteworthy that Buddhism, which represented many of the more popular philosophical ideas of the Hindūs, perhaps as early as the sixth century B.C., has more in common with the Sānkhya philosophy than with any of the other systems.

Even the cosmogony of Manu, although a compound of various theories, presents a process of evolution very similar to that of the Sānkhya.

Perhaps, however, the extreme popularity of the Sānkhyan idea of a union of two principles is best shown by the later cosmogony and mythology. In the Purāṇas and Tantras, the great repositories of the popular Hindū creed, Prakṛiti becomes a real mother of the universe, taking the form of female personifications, who are regarded as the wives or female energies and capacities (*śakti*) of the principal male deities, to whom, on the other hand, the name Purusha, in the sense of the Supreme Soul, or primeval male, is sometimes applied. This is especially the case, as we have shown in chapter ix., with the śakti, or female energy of Śiva, worshipped by vast numbers as the true 'mother of the universe.'[1]

From the popularity of the Sānhkya and its influence on the later mythology we shall not be surprised to find that there is a common saying in India,

[1] This is the best explanation of the fact, that the shrines of the *linga* and *yoni* are more common than any other throughout India.

'No knowledge equal to the Sānkhya, no power equal to the Yoga.'

4. *The Yoga.*

The Yoga, founded by Patanjali and regarded as a branch of the Sānkhya, is scarcely worthy of the name of a separate system of philosophy. Yet it has undoubted charms for the naturally contemplative and ascetical Hindū, and claims greater orthodoxy than the Sānkhya proper, by directly acknowledging the existence of a Supreme Being.

In brief, the aim of the Yoga is to teach the means by which the human soul may attain complete union with the Supreme Soul. This fusion or blending of the individual spirit (*jīvātman*) with Purusha, 'the universal Spirit,' may be effected even in the body by the constant habit of keeping the mind in its unmodified state—a state clear as crystal when uncoloured by contact with other substances, and by the practice of complete suppression of the passions (*vairāgya*). The last condition of suppression of all action is only to be achieved by meditation on the Supreme Being, who is defined to be 'a Spirit unaffected by works, having for one of his appellations the mystical monosyllable Om.' Indeed the repetition of *Om* is supposed to be all-efficacious in giving knowledge of the Supreme and preventing the obstacles to Yoga. The eight means of mental concentration are as follows :—

1. *Yama*, 'restraint.' 2. *Niyama*, 'religious observances.' 3. *Asana*, 'postures.' 4. *Prāṇāyāma*, 'suppression of the breath,' or 'breathing in a peculiar way.' 5. *Pratyāhāra*, 'restraint of the senses.' 6. *Dhāraṇa*, 'steadying of the mind.' 7. *Dhyāna*, 'contemplation.' 8. *Samādhi*, 'profound meditation,' or a state of religious trance, which is most effectually attained by such practices as fixing the eyes intently and incessantly on the tip of the nose, &c.

The Yoga system appears, in fact, to be a mere contrivance for getting rid of all thought, or rather for concentrating the mind with the utmost intensity upon nothing in particular. Ordinarily it is a strange compound of exercises, consisting in unnatural restraint, forced and painful postures, twistings and contortions of the limbs, suppressions of the breath undertaken apparently with no object except to achieve complete vacuity of mind. Many Hindū devotees and ascetics, especially those who, as forming a division of the Śaiva sect, identify the austere god Śiva with the Supreme Being, are commonly called Yogins or Yogīs, the professed object of their austerities being to effect union with the Deity.

6. *The Pūrva-Mīmānsā or Mīmānsā.*

The *Mīmānsā* of Jaimini is sometimes connected with the Vedānta, this latter being called the *Uttara-mīmānsā* or *Brahma-mīmānsā*, because founded on the Upanishads, or latter part of the Vedas, while Jaimini's system is styled either *Pūrva-mīmānsā*, 'an inquiry into the former portion of the Veda,' or *Karma-mīmānsā*, 'an inquiry into the ritual of the Veda,' because concerned with the Mantras and Brāhmaṇas only. It is more usual, however, to mark the opposition of the two systems to each other by calling the one Mīmānsā, and the other Vedānta. In real fact, the Mīmānsā is not a branch of any philosophical system: it is rather a system of Vedic interpretation. Its aim is to solve the doubts and discrepancies in regard to Vedic texts, caused by the discordant explanations of opposite schools; and its only claim to the title of a philosophy consists in its *mode* of interpretation. Its topics are arranged according to particular categories (such as, authoritativeness, indirect precept, &c.), and treated according to a kind of *logical method*, commencing with the proposition to be discussed, the doubt arising about it, the *Pūrva-paksha* or *primâ facie* and wrong view of the question, the *Uttara-paksha* or refutation of the wrong view, and the conclusion.

Its philosophical discussions amount to a kind of critical commentary on the Brāhmaṇa or ritual portion of the Veda; and it differs from the Vedānta in interpreting the Mantras according to the obvious literal sense, and not any supposed occult meaning underlying the text. Jaimini was, in real truth, the opponent of both rationalism and theism. Not that he denied a God, but the tendency of his teaching was to allow no voice or authority to either reason or God. The Veda was practically the only god. A Supreme Being might exist, but was not necessary to the system. The Veda, said Jaimini, is itself authority, and has no need of an authorizer. His first aphorism states the whole aim and object of his system, viz., a desire to know *Dharma* or duty, which consists in the performance of the rites and sacrifices prescribed by the Veda, because they are so prescribed, without reference to the will or approval of any personal god, for Dharma is itself the bestower of reward. Some recent Mīmānsakas, however, maintain that Dharma ought to be performed as an offering to a Supreme Being, and that it is to be so performed as a means of emancipation.

Some singular speculations occur in Jaimini's system. His belief in the inherent authority of the Veda, independently of any divine Revealer, leads him to assert its own absolute eternity, and he declares that only eternally pre-existing objects are mentioned in it. Other strange doctrines maintained by him are that there is a perpetual connection between a word and its sense, and that sound is eternal, or rather, that an eternal sound underlies all temporary sound.

We may add, in illustration of the notion of the eternity of sound, that the Chinese have a saying: 'The echoes of a word once uttered vibrate in space to all eternity.'

6. *The Vedānta.*

The Vedānta of Vyāsa or Bādarāyaṇa is, for convenience, placed last of the six orthodox systems; but on many accounts it ought to stand first. The outline of its pantheistic creed is traceable, as we have seen, in the Ṛig-veda, and it conforms more closely than any other system to the doctrines propounded in the Upanishads, on which treatises indeed, as forming the end of the Veda, it professes to be founded. Moreover, it is the truest exponent of the habits of thought of thoughtful Hindūs, as much in the most recent as in the most ancient times. The most celebrated teacher of this school of philosophy was Śankarāćārya (see p. 137), who was the great reviver of Brāhmanism, in opposition to unorthodox Buddhism, about the end of the 7th or beginning of the 8th century of our era.

As the Nyāya has much in common with the practical philosophy of Aristotle, which gave to things and individuals, rather than to ideas, a real existence, so the Vedānta offers many parallels to the idealism of Plato.

A Vedāntist's creed has the merit of extreme simplicity, being comprised in the well-known formula of three words from the C'hāndogya Upanishad (*ekam evādvitīyam*, one only essence without a second), or in the following: "Brahma exists truly, the world falsely, the soul is only Brahma, and no other," or in the following: "All this universe indeed is Brahma; from him does it proceed; into him is it dissolved; in him it breathes. So let every one adore him calmly."

Here, then, we have presented to us a different view of the origin of the world. In the Nyāya it proceeded from a concurrence of eternal atoms; in the Sānkhya from one original eternal element called Prakṛiti; both operating independently, though associated with eternal souls, and, according to one view, presided over by a supreme soul. But, in the Vedānta, there is really no material world at all, as distinct from the universal Soul. Hence, the doctrine of this school is called *A-dvaita*, 'non-dualism.' The universe exists, but merely as a form of the one eternal Essence.

Bādarāyaṇa's first aphorism states the object of the whole system in one word, viz., *Brahma-jijnāsā*, 'the desire of knowing Brahma' (neut.).

In the second aphorism this Brahma is defined to mean, 'that from which the production of this universe results.'

From other portions of the aphorisms it appears that the one universal essence, called Brahma (not *Brahmā*), is to the external world what yarn is to cloth, what milk to curds, what earth to a jar, what gold to a bracelet. This Essence is both creator and creation, actor and act. It is itself Existence, Knowledge, and Joy (*Saċ-ċid-ānanda*),[1] but at the same time, without parts, unbound by qualities, without action, without emotion, having no consciousness, such as is denoted by 'I' and 'Thou,' apprehending no person or thing, nor apprehended by any, having neither beginning nor end, immutable, the only real entity.

---

[1] This is the Vedāntist's trinity, corresponding very remarkably, as Mr. Robson observes, with the Author of Existence (the Father), the Source of Wisdom (Christ, the Word), and the Source of Joy (the Holy Spirit); thus the Veda, the Vedānta, and the Bhakti-śāstras all point to the triple nature of the Supreme Being.

If this be true, then pure Being must be almost identical with pure Nothing, so that the two extremes of Buddhistic Nihilism and Vedāntic Pantheism, far as they profess to be apart, appear in the end to meet.

The creed of the Vedāntist does not necessarily imply that the world is all Māyā, 'mere illusion.' A true Vedāntist, though he affirms that Brahma alone is real, allows a practical (*vyāvahārika*) existence to souls, the world, and Iśvara, as distinguished from real (*pāramārthika*) and from illusory existence (*prātibhāsika*). How, indeed, can it be denied that external things exist when we see them and feel them at every instant? But how, on the other hand, can it be maintained that an impure world is evolved from a pure spiritual essence? To avoid this difficulty, the Supreme Spirit is represented as ignoring himself by a sort of self-imposed ignorance, in order to draw out from himself, for his own amusement, the separate individuated souls and various appearances, which, although really parts of his own essence, constitute the apparent phenomena of the universe. Hence the external world, individual souls, and even Iśvara, the personal God, are all described as created by a power which the Vedāntist is obliged, for want of a better solution of his difficulty, to call *A-vidyā*, generally translated 'Ignorance,' but perhaps better rendered by 'False Knowledge,' or 'False Notion.'

Of this power there are two distinct forms of operation, that of envelopment (*āvaraṇa*), and that of projection (*vikshepa*); which last projects on the soul the appearance of a world, producing first the five subtle elements, and drawing out from them seventeen subtle bodies (comprising the five organs of sense, the five organs of action, the five vital airs, with *buddhi* and *manas*), and the five gross elements, as in the Sānkhya.

By reason of Avidyā, then, the Jīvātman, or living soul of every individual, mistakes the world as well as its own body and mind for realities, just as a rope in a dark night might be mistaken for a snake. The moment the personal soul is set free from this self-imposed ignorance by a proper understanding of the truth through the Vedānta philosophy, all the illusion vanishes, and the identity of the Jīvātman and of the whole phenomenal universe with the Paramātman, or Supreme Soul, is re-established.

It may be noted that in the Vedānta the living soul of individuals, when separated off from the Supreme Soul, is regarded as enclosed in a succession of cases (*kośa*) which envelop it, and, as it were, fold one over the other, like the coats of an onion.[1]

Of course the Vedānta theory, if pushed to its ultimate consequences, must lead to the neglect of all duties, religious and moral, of all activity, physical and intellectual, and of all self-culture. If everything be God, then you and he and I must be one. Why should any efforts be made for the advancement of self or for the good of others? Everything we have must be common property.

Eclectic School.—The Bhagavad-Gītā.

The Bhagavad-gītā,[2] commented on by the great Vedāntic teacher Śankarāćārya (see pp. 83, 203), may

---

[1] These are called *Vijnāna-maya*, *Mano-maya*, *Prāṇa-maya*, *Anna-maya*, and a fifth is sometimes named *Ānanda-maya*.

[2] I am obliged to repeat here, as in some of the preceding pages of this work, much of what I have already described in the work called 'Indian Wisdom,' for the simple reason that it is essential to my present subject; and I find myself unable to vary my descriptions without spoiling them.

be regarded as representing the Eclectic school of Indian philosophy. As the regular systems were developments of the Upanishads, so the Eclectic school is connected with those mystical treatises through the Śvetāśvatara Upanishad. This last is a comparatively modern Upanishad, but whether it was composed before or after the Bhagavad-gītā, the design of both is evidently the same. They both aim at reconciling the conflicting views of different systems, by an attempt to engraft the Sānkhya and Yoga upon Vedānta doctrines. Although, therefore, the order of creation and much of the cosmogony of the Sānkhya system are retained in both, the sovereignty of the Supreme Soul of the universe (*Brahman*, neut.) with which Kṛishṇa is identified, as the source and end of all created things, and yet wholly independent of all such creations, is asserted by both.

The real author of the Bhagavad-gītā is unknown. Nor is it known when the work was inserted in the Bhīshma-pārvan of the Mahā-bhārata, in which poem it lies inlaid like a pearl, contributing, with other numerous episodes, to the tesselated character of that immense epic.[1]

The author was probably an earnest Brāhman and nominally a Vaishṇava, but really a philosopher whose mind was cast in a broad mould. He is supposed to have lived in India about the second or third century of our era. Finding no rest for his spirit in the extreme dogmatism of any one system of philosophy, as commonly taught in his own time, much less in the narrow-minded exclusiveness, and corrupt forms of Brāhmanism which surrounded him, he was driven to construct an eclectic school of his

[1] It commences at line 830 of the 25th chapter of the Parvan, and ends at line 1,532.

own. This he has done with great perspicuity and beauty of language in the Bhagavad-gītā, combining various theories into one system, by interweaving, so to speak, threads from the Sānkhya, Yoga, and Vedānta, so as to form a many-coloured woof of thought, which is shot across a stiff warp of the doctrine of faith (*bhakti*) in Kṛishṇa, and of stern devotion to caste duties (*dharma*). Of these cross threads the most conspicuous are those of the Sānkhya, for which the author of the Gītā has an evident predilection. As a necessary result of its composite character, the work is, of course, full of inconsistencies. The whole composition is skilfully thrown into the form of a dramatic poem, something after the manner of the book of Job or a dialogue of Plato. The speakers are the two most important personages in the Mahābhārata—Arjuna and Kṛishṇa. Arjuna is, perhaps, the real hero of that epic. He is the bravest, and yet the most tender-hearted of the five sons of Pāṇḍu. The god Kṛishṇa, who is identified with Vishṇu, and in this philosophical dialogue is held to be the Supreme Being himself, had taken form as the son of Devakī and Vasudeva, who was brother of Kuntī, wife of Pāṇḍu. Hence the god was cousin of the sons of Pāṇḍu, brother of Dhṛita-rāshṭra, the sons of these brothers being of course related as cousins to each other. In the great war which arose between the two families of Pāṇḍu and Dhṛita-rāshṭra (see p. 112), representing two Kshatriya races contending for supremacy, Kṛishṇa refused to take up arms on either side, but consented to act as the charioteer of Arjuna, and to aid him with his advice. At the commencement of the Bhagavad-gītā the two contending armies are supposed to be drawn up in battle-array, when Arjuna is struck with sudden compunction at the idea of fighting his way to a kingdom through the blood of his kindred, and asks Kṛishna's opinion as to his proper course of action. Kṛishṇa's reply is made the occasion of the long philosophical dialogue, commonly called 'the Song of the Adorable One,' supposed to contain the actual utterances of the god, and venerated as one of the most sacred portions of Indian literature, as it certainly is one of the most beautiful. Undoubtedly the main design of the poem, the sentiments expressed in which have exerted a powerful influence throughout India for the last 1600 years, is to inculcate the doctrine of *Bhakti*, to exalt the duties of caste above all other obligations, including those of friendship and kindred. As Arjuna belongs to the military caste, he is exhorted to perform his appointed work as a soldier. Again and again is he urged to fight, without the least thought about consequences, and without the slightest question as to the propriety of slaughtering his relations. Hence we have the following sentiments often repeated (III. 35, XVIII. 47, 48):

> Better to do the duty of one's caste,
> Though bad and ill-performed and fraught with evil,
> Than undertake the business of another,
> However good it be. For better far
> Abandon life at once than not fulfil
> One's own appointed work; another's duty
> Brings danger to the man who meddles with it.
> Perfection is alone attained by him
> Who swerves not from the business of his caste.

The poem is divided into three sections, each containing six chapters, the philosophical teaching in each section being somewhat distinct.

The first section dwells chiefly on the benefits of the Yoga system, pointing out, however, that the asceticism and self-mortification of the Yoga ought to be joined with action, and the performance of caste duties, and winding up with a declaration that the grand aim of all self-suppression is to attain that most desirable state which enables a man to annihilate his own individuality, and see God in everything and everything in God. Arjuna is comforted under the distressing thought that he is about to kill his relations, by an argument drawn from the eternal existence of the soul, which is nobly expressed thus :

"The wise grieve not for the departed, nor for those who yet survive. Never was the time when I was not, nor thou, nor yonder chiefs, and never shall be the time when all of us shall not be ; as the embodied soul in this corporeal frame moves swiftly on through boyhood, youth, and age, so will it pass through other forms hereafter—be not grieved thereat. The man whom pain and pleasure, heat and cold affect not, he is fit for immortality. Whatever is not cannot be ; whatever is can never cease to be. Know this—the Being that spread this universe is indestructible. Who can destroy the Indestructible? These bodies that enclose the everlasting soul, inscrutable, immortal, have an end ; but he who thinks the soul can be destroyed, and he who deems it a destroyer, are alike mistaken ; it kills not, and is not killed ; it is not born, nor doth it ever die ; it has no past nor future—unproduced, unchanging, infinite ; he who knows it fixed, unborn, imperishable, indissoluble, how can that man destroy another, or extinguish ought below? As men abandon old and threadbare clothes to put on others new, so casts the embodied soul its worn-out frame to enter other forms. No dart can pierce it ; flame cannot consume it, water wet it not, nor scorching breezes dry it—indestructible, incapable of heat or moisture or aridity, eternal, all-pervading, steadfast, immovable, perpetual, yet imperceptible, incomprehensible, unfading, deathless, unimaginable."

In the second and sixth chapters the duty of Yoga or 'intense concentration of the mind on one subject' (viz. the Supreme Being, here identified with Kṛishṇa), till at last the great end of freedom from all thought, perfect calm, and absorption in the Deity are obtained, is enjoined with much force of language, as may be seen from the following extracts :

That holy man who stands immovable,
As if erect upon a pinnacle,[1]

[1] *Kūṭa-stha* (VI. 8) may mean 'standing erect like a peak.'

His appetites and organs all subdued,
Sated with knowledge secular and sacred,
To whom a lump of earth, a stone, or gold,
To whom friends, relatives, acquaintances,
Neutrals and enemies, the good and bad,
Are all alike, is called 'one yoked with God.'
The man who aims at that supreme condition
Of perfect yoking[2] with the Deity
Must first of all be moderate in all things,
In food, in sleep, in vigilance, in action,
In exercise and recreation. Then
Let him, if seeking God by deep abstraction,
Abandon his possessions and his hopes,
Betake himself to some secluded spot,[3]
And fix his heart and thoughts on God alone.
There let him choose a seat, not high nor low,
And with a cloth or skin to cover him,
And Kuśa grass beneath him, let him sit
Firm and erect, his body, head, and neck
Straight and immovable, his eyes directed
Towards a single point,[4] not looking round,
Devoid of passion, free from anxious thought,
His heart restrained, and deep in meditation.
E'en as a tortoise draws its head and feet
Within its shell, so must he keep his organs
Withdrawn from sensual objects. He whose senses
Are well controlled attains to sacred knowledge,
And thence obtains tranquillity of thought.
Without quiescence there can be no bliss.
E'en as a storm-tossed ship upon the waves,
So is the man whose heart obeys his passions,
Which, like the winds, will hurry him away.
Quiescence is the state of the Supreme.
He who, intent on meditation, joins

---

[1] Tersely expressed in Sanskrit by *sama-loshṭāśma-kāñćana* (VI. 8).

[2] I use these expressions as kindred words to the Sanskrit *yukta* and *yoga*. 'Joined' and 'junction' are also cognate expressions.

[3] Cf. Matt. vi. 6: 'But thou, when thou prayest, enter into thy closet, and when thou hast shut thy door, pray to thy Father which is in secret.'

[4] The text (VI. 13) says, 'fixing his eyes on the tip of his nose' (*samprekshya nāsikāgram*).

His soul with the Supreme, is like a flame
That flickers not when sheltered from the wind.

In the second division of this poem the pantheistic doctrines of the Vedānta are more directly inculcated than in the other sections. Kṛishṇa here, in the plainest language, claims adoration as one with the great universal spirit, pervading and constituting the universe.

The following are portions from different parts of this section:

Whate'er thou dost perform, whate'er thou eatest,
Whate'er thou givest to the poor, whate'er
Thou offerest in sacrifice, whate'er
Thou doest as an act of holy penance,
Do all as if to me, O Arjuna (IX. 27).[1]
I am the ancient Sage, without beginning,
I am the Ruler and the All-sustainer,
I am incomprehensible in form,
More subtle and minute than subtlest atoms;
I am the cause of the whole universe;

---

[1] Compare 1 Cor. x. 31: 'Whether therefore ye eat, or drink, or whatsoever ye do, do all to the glory of God.' Dr. Lorinser, expanding the views of Professor Weber and others concerning the influence of Christianity on the legends of Kṛishṇa, thinks that many of the sentiments of the Bhagavad-gītā have been directly borrowed from the New Testament, copies of which, he thinks, found their way into India about the third century, when he believes the poem to have been written. He even adopts the theory of a parallel in the names of Christ and Kṛishṇa. He does not, however, sufficiently bear in mind that fragments of truth are to be found in all religious systems, however false, and that the Bible, though a true revelation, is still, in regard to the human mind, through which the thoughts are transfused, a thoroughly Oriental book, cast in an Oriental mould, and full of Oriental ideas and expressions. Some of his comparisons seem mere coincidences of language, which might occur independently. Nevertheless, something may be said for Dr. Lorinser's theory. His German translation (1869) is rich in notes, pointing out parallels.' See also the 'Indian Antiquary' for October, 1873.

Through me it is created and dissolved ;
On me all things within it hang suspended,
Like pearls upon a string.[1] I am the light
In sun and moon, far, far beyond the darkness ;[2]
I am the brilliancy in flame, the radiance
In all that's radiant, and the light of lights,
The sound in ether, fragrance in the earth,
The seed eternal of existing things,[3]
The life in all, the father, mother, husband,
Forefather, and sustainer of the world,
Its friend and lord. I am its way[4] and refuge,
Its habitation and receptacle,
I am its witness. I am Victory
And Energy ; I watch the universe
With eyes and face in all directions turned.
I dwell, as Wisdom, in the heart of all.
I am the Goodness of the good, I am
Beginning, Middle, End, eternal Time,
The Birth, the Death of all.[5] I am the symbol A
Among the characters. I have created all
Out of one portion of myself. E'en those
Who are of low and unpretending birth,[6]
May find the path to highest happiness,
If they depend on me ; how much more those
Who are by rank and penance holy Brāhmans
And saintly soldier-princes like thyself.
Then be not sorrowful ; from all thy sins
I will deliver thee.[7] Think thou on me,

---

[1] Compare Rom. xi. 36 : 'Of Him, and through Him, and unto Him, are all things.' John i. 3 : 'All things were made by Him; and without Him was not anything made that was made.'

[2] Compare 1 John i. 5 : 'God is light, and in Him is no darkness at all.'

[3] Compare John i. 3 : 'All things were made by Him.'

[4] Cf. John xiv. 6 : 'I am the way.'

[5] Compare Rev. i. 17, 18 : 'I am the first and the last ; and have the keys of hell and of death.'

[6] The text states who these are; viz. women, Vaiśyas, and S'ūdras. This is significant in regard to the Hindū estimate of the female sex. A woman's religion is thought to consist in obedience, first to her father, and then to her husband, with attention to domestic duties.

[7] Cf. Matt. ix. 2 : 'Be of good cheer ; thy sins be forgiven

Have faith in me, adore and worship me,[1]
And join thyself in meditation to me;
Thus shalt thou come to me, O Arjuna;
Thus shalt thou rise to my supreme abode,
Where neither sun nor moon hath need to shine,
For know that all the lustre they possess is mine.[2]

We come now to Chapter XI., called 'the Vision (or Revelation) of the Universal Form' (*viśva-rūpa-darśana*). Arjuna, filled with awe at the discovery of the true nature of Kṛishṇa, acting as his charioteer, addresses him thus:

Most mighty Lord supreme, this revelation
Of thy mysterious essence and thy oneness
With the eternal Spirit, clears away
The mists of my illusions. Show me then
Thy form celestial, most divine of men,
If haply I may dare to look upon it.

To this Kṛishṇa replies:

Thou canst not bear to gaze upon my shape
With these thy human eyes, O son of Pāṇḍu,
But now I gift thee with celestial vision;
Behold me in a hundred thousand forms,
In phases, colours, fashions infinite.

Then follows the description of Kṛishṇa's supernatural transformation:[3]

---

thee.' A sense of original corruption seems to be felt by all classes of Hindūs, as indicated by the following prayer used after the Gāyatrī by some Vaishṇavas:—

Pāpo 'ham pāpa-karmāham pāpātmā pāpa-sambhavaḥ,
Trāhi mām, puṇḍarīkāksha sarva-pāpa-hara Hare,

'I am sinful, I commit sin, my nature is sinful, I am conceived in sin;
Save me, O thou lotus-eyed Hari, the remover of sin.'

[1] Cf. Prov. xxiii. 26: 'My son, give me thine heart.'

[2] Cf. Rev. xxi. 23: 'The city had no need of the sun, neither of the moon, to shine in it; for the glory of God did lighten it.'

[3] The idea of this Dr. Lorinser considers borrowed from the Gospel narrative of the transfiguration. It is certainly very in-

Thus having said, the mighty Lord of all
Displayed to Arjuna his form supreme,
Endowed with countless mouths and countless eyes,
With countless faces turned to every quarter,
With countless marvellous appearances,
With ornaments, and wreaths, and robes divine,
With heavenly fragrance and celestial weapons.
It was as if the firmament were filled,
All in an instant with a thousand suns,
Blazing with dazzling lustre, so beheld he
The glories of the universe collected
In the one person of the God of gods.[1]

Arjuna with every hair on his body bristling with awe, bows his head at this vision, and folding his hands in reverence, gives utterance to a passionate outburst of enthusiastic adoration, which is here abridged :

I see thee, mighty Lord of all, revealed
In forms of infinite diversity.
I see thee like a mass of purest light,
Flashing thy lustre everywhere around.
I see thee crowned with splendour like the sun,
Pervading earth and sky, immeasurable,
Boundless, without beginning, middle, end,
Preserver of imperishable law,
The everlasting Man ;[2] the triple world
Is awe-struck at this vision of thy form,
Stupendous, indescribable in glory.
Have mercy, God of gods ; the universe
Is fitly dazzled by thy majesty,
Fitly to thee alone devotes its homage.

---

structive to contrast the simplicity of the Gospel scene : 'His face did shine as the sun, and his raiment was white as the light' (Matt. xvii. 2 ; Mark ix. 3).

[1] In the Udyoga-parvan of the Mahā-bhārata (4419–4430) Kṛishṇa reveals his form in the same way to the assembled princes, who are obliged to close their eyes at the awful sight, while the blind Dhṛita-rāshṭra is gifted with divine vision that he may behold the glorious spectacle (4437).

[2] *Sanātanaḥ purushaḥ* (XI. 18) may be translated 'the eternal Spirit.'

At thy approach the evil demons flee,
Scattered in terror to the winds of heaven.
The multitude of holy saints[1] adore thee—
Thee, first Creator,[2] lord of all the gods,
The ancient One,[3] supreme Receptacle
Of all that is and is not, knowing all,
And to be known by all. Immensely vast,
Thou comprehendest all, thou art the All (XI. 40).
To thee earth's greatest heroes must return,
Blending once more with thy resplendent essence,
Like mighty rivers rushing to the ocean (XI. 28).
To thee be sung a thousand hymns of praise
By every creature and from every quarter,
Before, above, behind. Hail! Hail! thou All!
Again and yet again I worship thee.
Have mercy, I implore thee, and forgive,
That I, in ignorance of this thy glory,
Presumed to call thee Friend; and pardon too
Whate'er I have too negligently uttered,
Addressing thee in too familiar tones.
Unrivalled God of gods, I fall before thee
Prostrate in adoration, thou the Father
Of all that lives and lives not; have compassion,
Bear with me, as a father with a son,
Or as a lover with a cherished one.
Now that I see thee as thou really art,
I thrill with terror! Mercy! Lord of lords,
Once more display to me thy human form,
Thou habitation of the universe.[4]

Many other remarkable passages might be adduced in connection with the first two divisions of the sub-

---

[1] Cf. parts of the Te Deum. The Siddhas form a group (*gaṇa*) of semi-divine beings, supposed to possess great purity, called Sādhyas in the earlier mythology (Manu, i. 22). Siddhas and Sādhyas are sometimes confused, though here mentioned separately (see p. 167).

[2] Cf. John viii. 58: 'Before Abraham was, I am.'

[3] *Purushaḥ purāṇaḥ*, 'the most ancient person' (XI. 38). Cf. Daniel vii. 9: 'The Ancient of days did sit.'

[4] XI. 45, 46. Dr. Lorinser compares the awe of our Lord's disciples (Matt. xvii. 6): 'They fell on their face, and were sore afraid.' Also of Simon Peter (Luke v. 8): 'When Simon Peter saw it, he fell down at Jesus' knees, saying, Depart from me; for I am a sinful man, O Lord.'

ject matter of the Bhagavad-gītā. The following may be noted:

He who has brought his members under subjection, but sits with foolish mind thinking in his heart of sensual things, is called a hypocrite (III. 6. Cf. Matt. v. 28).

Many are my births that are past; many are thine too, O Arjuna. I know them all, but thou knowest them not (IV. 5. Cf. John viii. 14).

For the establishment of righteousness am I born from time to time (IV. 8. Cf. John xviii. 37; 1 John iii. 3).

I am dearer to the wise than all possessions, and he is dear to me (VI. 17. Cf. Luke xiv. 33; John xiv. 21).

The ignorant, the unbeliever, and he of a doubting mind perish utterly (IV. 40. Cf. Mark xvi. 16).

In him are all beings, by him this universe was spread out (VIII. 22. Cf. Acts xvii. 28).

Deluded men despise me when I have taken human form (IX. 11. Cf. John i. 10).

In all the Vedas I am to be known (XV. 15. Cf. John v. 39).

As many uses as there are in a reservoir filled with waters coming from all parts (for bathing, washing, or drinking), so many does a knowing Brāhman find in all the Vedas (II. 46).

There will be found an obvious similarity if we compare with the last statement, which is certainly borne out by the practice of the present day, the various uses made of texts from our own sacred Scriptures by persons who wish to find authority for extreme opinions.

The next passage is suggestive of the doctrine that the condition of the soul for a future state is determined before death:

Whatever a man's state of mind be at the moment when he leaves the body, to that condition does he always go, being made to conform to that (VIII. 6. Cf. Eccles. xi. 3). This is called the dying Sanskāra which delays the passage to heaven.

A similar passage occurs in the C'hāndogya Upanishad, as follows:

Man is a creature of intelligence (*kratu-maya*), whatever ideas he forms in this life, he becomes so when he departs to another, therefore he should reflect on God (III. 14, 1).

Subjoined is a paraphrase of another remarkable passage of the Bhagavad-gītā (XVI. 12–16). It may be compared with Luke xii. 17–20:

> Entangled in a hundred worldly snares,
> Self-seeking men, by ignorance deluded,
> Strive by unrighteous means to pile up riches.
> Then, in their self-complacency, they say,
> 'This acquisition I have made to-day,
> That I will gain to-morrow; so much pelf
> Is hoarded up already, so much more
> Remains that I have yet to treasure up.
> This enemy I have destroyed, him also,
> And others in their turn I will dispatch.
> I am a lord; I will enjoy myself;
> I'm wealthy, noble, strong, successful, happy;
> I'm absolutely perfect; no one else
> In all the world can be compared to me.
> Now I will offer up a sacrifice,
> Give gifts with lavish hand and be triumphant.'
> Such men, befooled by endless, vain conceits,
> Caught in the meshes of the world's illusion,
> Immersed in sensuality, descend
> Down to the foulest hell of unclean spirits.

A few lines from Chapter III. may be added, in which Kṛishṇa exhorts Arjuna to energetic action by an argument drawn from the example set by himself in his own everlasting exertions for the good of the world (cf. John v. 17). The order of the text is not observed in the following version, and the sentiment in lines 6, 7, is from Chapter II. 47:

> Perform all necessary acts, for action
> Is better than inaction, none can live
> By sitting still and doing nought; it is
> By action only that a man attains
> Immunity from action. Yet in working
> Ne'er work for recompense; let the act's motive
> Be in the act itself. Know that work
> Proceeds from the Supreme. I am the pattern
> For man to follow; know that I have done

All acts already, nought remains for me
To gain by action, yet I work for ever
Unweariedly, and this whole universe
Would perish if I did not work my work (III. 19).

The third division of the poem, comprising the last six chapters, aims particularly at interweaving Sānkhya doctrines with the Vedānta, though this is done more or less throughout the whole work. It accepts the doctrine of a supreme presiding spirit, as the first source of the universe, and asserts that both Prakṛiti and Purusha—that is, the original eternal element and soul—both emanate from this Supreme Being. Moreover, it maintains the individuality of souls, and affirms that the body and all the world of sense is evolved out of Prakṛiti by the regular Sānkhyan process, through Buddhi, Ahan-kāra, the five subtile elements, the five grosser elements, and the eleven organs, including mind.

Thus in XIII. 19, and in VII. 4–6, we read:

Learn that *Prakṛiti* and *Purusha* also are both of them without beginning. And know that the Vikāras, or 'productions,' and the Guṇas are sprung from Prakṛiti.

Earth, water, fire, air, ether, mind, intellect, and egoism, into these eight is my Prakṛiti divided. This Prakṛiti is the inferior one, but learn my superior Prakṛiti to be other than this. Understand that all things are produced from this other Prakṛiti.

Again, in VII. 12–14, Kṛishṇa, speaking of the three Guṇas, says:

Know that all the three Guṇas, whether Sattva, Rajas, or Tamas, proceed only from me. I am not in them, but they in me.

All this universe, deluded by these three conditions consisting of the Guṇas, does not recognize me, the imperishable Being, superior to them all.

For this divine illusion (*Māyā*, i.e. 'illusory creation'), consisting of the three Guṇas, caused by me, is difficult to be passed over. Those only are delivered from it who have recourse to me.

The eclecticism of the Bhagavad-gītā will be sufficiently apparent from these examples. Three or four passages (taken from Chapter III. 27, Chapter XIII. 29, 31) will form a fit conclusion to the subject, as they contain the gist of the whole argument, viz. that it is Arjuna's duty, as a soldier, to act like a soldier, and to do the work of his caste, regardless of consequences; and that this may be done consistently with adhesion to the Vedāntic dogma of the soul's real inactivity and state of passionless repose:

All actions are incessantly performed
By operation of the qualities
Of Prakṛiti; deluded by the thought
Of individuality, the soul
Vainly believes itself to be the doer.
The soul existing from eternity,
Devoid of qualities, imperishable,
Abiding in the body, yet supreme,
Acts not, nor is by any act polluted.
He who perceives that actions are performed
By Prakṛiti alone, and that the soul
Is not an actor, sees the truth aright.

Kṛishṇa's last advice may be thus summed up:

Act then and do thine own appointed task,
In every action my assistance ask,
Do all with heart and soul absorbed in me,
So shalt thou gain thine end and be from trouble free.

Arjuna's conclusion may be thus paraphrased:

Eternal One! thy glory just beheld
Has all illusion from my soul dispelled;
Now by thy favour is my conscience clear,
I will thy bidding do and fight without a fear.

This beautiful poem offers, as we have seen, numerous parallels to passages in our own sacred Scriptures. But if we examine the writings and recorded sayings of three great Roman philosophers, Seneca, Epictetus, and Marcus Aurelius, we shall find them also full of similar resemblances, while there appears to be no ground whatever for supposing that these eminent Pagan writers and thinkers derived any of their ideas from either Jewish or Christian sources.

The fact is that we have not sufficient data for determining how far the presence of corrupt forms of Christianity in particular districts of India from early times, has affected Hindūism. The Hindū system is like a vast ocean which has received an infinite number of streams, and all we can say is that into some of these streams Christian tributaries, from turbid springs, which have afterwards dried up, may possibly have found their way and become absorbed.[1]

Jainism.

Jainism is the only representative of Buddhistic ideas now left in India, and has so much in common with them that, having already glanced at the chief features of Buddhism (see Chapter VI.), we need only notice a few of the distinctive traits of a system which is certainly the near relation of Buddhism, if not its actual descendant.

The Jainas, who are still found in great numbers in various parts of India (especially on the western coast), are divided into two principal sects:—1. The Śvetāmbaras, 'clothed in white garments'; 2. the Digambaras, 'sky-clad,' or 'naked'; the latter, however, wear coloured garments, except while eating. These sects, though their doctrines rest on nearly the same sacred books, called collectively Āgamas, and classed under the head of Angas, Upāngas, &c.,[2] differ in

[1] M. de Thevenot, who visited Agra in 1666, wrote that 'some affirm that there are 25,000 Christian families in Agra.' In all probability, Shah Jahān employed only Europeans for his arsenals, artillery, &c. See Sleeman's Rambles, vol. ii. p. 49.

[2] According to Rājendralāla Mitra, the Jaina scriptures are

some unimportant matters, such as the clothing or non-clothing of their images, the number of their heavens, &c. They both agree with the Buddhists in rejecting the Veda of the Brāhmans. The principal point in the Jaina creed is the reverence paid to holy men, who, by long discipline, have raised themselves to divine perfection. The Jina, or 'conquering saint, who has conquered all worldly desires' (whence the adjective Jaina, to denote a follower of the Jinas), is with Jainas what the Buddha, or 'perfectly enlightened saint,' is with Bauddhas. He is also called Jineśvara, 'chief of the Jinas'; Arhat, 'the venerable'; Tīrthakara, 'the saint who has made the passage of the world'; Sarva-jna, 'omniscient'; Bhagavat, 'holy one.' Time with Jainas proceeds in two eternally recurring cycles of immense duration, defying all human calculation: 1. the Utsarpiṇī or 'ascending cycle'; 2. Avasarpiṇi or 'descending cycle.' Each of these had six stages. Those of the Utsarpiṇī period are bad-bad, bad, bad-good, good-bad, good, good-good time. In the Avasarpiṇī period, the series begins with good-good and goes regularly backwards. In the first cycle the age and stature of men increase; in the other decrease. We are now

---

comprised in fifty different works, collectively called the *Sūtras*, and sometimes the *Siddhāntas*, and classed in two different ways: 1st, under the two heads of *Kalpa-sūtra* and *Agama*, five works coming under the former, and forty-five under the latter head. 2ndly, under eight different heads, viz. 1. eleven *Angas*; 2. twelve *Upāngas*; 3. four *Mūla-sūtra*; 4. five *Kalpa-sūtra*; 5. six *Cheddas*; 6. ten *Payannas*; 7. *Nandi-sūtra*; 8. *Anuyoga-dvāra-sūtra*. Some of them have a fourfold commentary, under the names *Ṭīkā*, *Niryukti*, *Cūrṇī*, and *Bhāshya*, constituting with the original the fivefold (*pañcānga*) Sūtra. They are partly in Sanskṛit, partly in Māgadhī Prākṛit, and the total of the fifty works is said to amount to 600,000 S'lokas (see Notices of Sanskṛit MSS. No. VIII. p. 67).

in the fifth stage of the Avasarpiṇī, *i.e.* in 'bad' time. When the two cycles have run out, a Yuga or age is accomplished. Twenty-four Jinas, or 'perfect saints,' raised to the rank of gods, have appeared in the present Avasarpiṇī cycle, twenty-four in the past Utsarpiṇī, and twenty-four will appear in the future. The idols representing them are always, like that of Buddha, in a contemplative posture. The first Jina of the present cycle lived 8,400,000 years, and attained a stature equal to the length of 500 bows (*dhanus*). The age and stature of the second were somewhat less; and so in a descending scale. The last two Jinas, Pārśva-nātha and Mahā-vīra, were probably real persons, and are those principally revered by the Jainas of the present day. In all likelihood the first founder of the sect was Pārśva-nātha, and its first active propagator Mahā-vīra. In the same cycle there have lived twelve 'Cakra-vartins, 'universal emperors,' nine divine personages called Bala-devas, nine called Vāsudevas, and nine others called Prativāsudevas, making a list of sixty-three divine persons in all.

With regard to the world, the Jainas affirm that, being formed of eternal atoms, it has existed and will exist eternally. They believe that it has three divisions, viz. lower, middle, and upper, and that there are numerous hells and heavens. All existing things are arranged under the two great Tattvas of Jīva, 'living soul,' and A-jīva, 'inanimate objects.' Of living souls there are three kinds: *a. Nitya-siddha*, 'ever perfect,' as the Jina; *b. Muktātman*, 'liberated soul'; *c. Baddhātman*, 'bound soul,' or one bound by works and worldly associations. Material objects are sometimes classed under a Tattva called *Pudgala*, and some make seven, others nine Tattvas.

There are three 'gems,' which together effect the soul's liberation (*moksha*); viz. *a.* right intuition, *b.* right knowledge, *c.* right conduct. This last consists in observing five duties or vows of self-restraint, thus :

1. Do not kill or injure. Strict Jainas carry this to so preposterous an extreme that they strain water before drinking it, sweep the ground with a brush before treading on it, never eat or drink in the dark, and sometimes wear muslin before their mouths to prevent the risk of swallowing minute insects. Moreover, they never eat figs or any fruit containing seed, nor will they even touch flesh-meat with their hands. 2. Do not tell lies. 3. Steal not. 4. Be chaste and temperate in thought, word, and deed. 5. Desire nothing immoderately.

There are two classes of Jainas, as of Buddhists; viz. *S'rāvakas*, those who engage in secular occupations, and *Yatis*, monks or ascetics, who are required to pluck out their hair or wear it cropped short. The latter often congregate in Maṭhas or 'monasteries,' being called Sādhu when not monastic.

It should be noted that most Jainas have a sort of modified belief in the Hindū gods, especially Brahmā, Vishṇu, Śiva, and Gaṇeśa, with their consorts, as beings subordinated to the Jainas; and representations of these deities are sometimes observable in the precincts of their temples. They are even observers of caste practices, and claim to be regarded as Hindūs, though rejecting the Hindū Veda. In Western India the priests of some Jaina temples are said to be Brāhmans.

The Ćārvākas.

There is no such philosophical sect as that of the Ćārvākas at present in India, but that a materialistic school of thinkers so called once existed, and exercised no slight influence on sceptical philosophy, is proved by the frequent allusions to them in Indian writings. No account of Hindūism, therefore, would be complete without a brief statement of their opinions.

Nothing is known about C'ārvāka, the founder of

this materialistic school. He may be styled the Indian Pyrrho or Epicurus, and his system is the worst form of all heresies. On that account, perhaps, it was honoured with the first place in Mādhavāćārya's compendium of all the philosophical systems, called Sarva-darśana-sangraha. In the Śānti-parvan of the Mahābhārata (1410, &c.) there is a story of a Rākshasa named C'ārvāka, who, in the disguise of a mendicant Brāhman, reviled Yudhishṭhira during his triumphant entry into Hastinā-pura, and uttered profane and heretical doctrines. He was, however, soon detected, and the real Brāhmans, filled with fury, killed him on the spot. This legend may possibly rest on some basis of fact.

The creed of the C'ārvākas, who are sometimes called Lokāyatas or Lokāyatikas,[1] is said to have been derived from the Vārhaspatya Sūtras (Aphorisms of Vṛihaspati). They reject all the Pramāṇas, or 'sources of true knowledge,' except Pratyaksha, 'perception by the senses' (see p. 188); they admit only four Tattvas or 'eternal principles,' viz. earth, air, fire, and water; and from these intelligence (*ćaitanya*) is alleged to be produced; they affirm that the soul is not different from the body; and, lastly, they assert that all the phenomena of the world are spontaneously produced, without even the help of Adṛishṭa (see p. 51). Their views may be summed up with a version of a passage in the Sarva-darśana-sangraha, setting forth their opinions according to the supposed teaching of Vṛihaspati. The sentiments, it will be perceived, are worthy of the most sceptical, materialistic, and epicurean of European writers:

No heaven exists, no final liberation,
No soul, no other world, no rights of caste,

---

[1] By some this name is given to a subdivision of the C'ārvākas, or the materialistic school.

No recompense for acts ; the Agnihotra,
The triple Veda, triple self-command,[1]
And all the dust and ashes of repentance—
These yield a means of livelihood for men
Devoid of intellect and manliness.
If victims slaughtered at a sacrifice
Are raised to heavenly mansions,[2] why should not
The sacrificer immolate his father?
If offerings of food can satisfy[3]
Hungry departed spirits, why supply
The man who goes a journey with provisions?
His friends at home can feed him with oblations.
If those abiding in celestial spheres
Are filled with food presented upon earth,
Why should not those who live in upper stories
Be nourished by a meal spread out below?
While life endures, let life be spent in ease
And merriment ;[4] let a man borrow money
From all his friends and feast on melted butter.
How can this body when reduced to dust
Revisit earth? and if a ghost can pass
To other worlds, why does not strong affection
For those he leaves behind attract him back?
The costly rites enjoined for those who die
Are a mere means of livelihood devised
By sacerdotal cunning—nothing more.
The three composers of the triple Veda
Were rogues, or evil spirits, or buffoons.
The recitation of mysterious words
And jabber[5] of the priests is simple nonsense.

---

[1] *Tri-daṇḍa*, 'control over thoughts, words, and actions, denoted by the three Daṇḍas or staves carried by ascetics.' See Manu, XII. 10, 11.

[2] See Manu, V. 42, and p. 38 of this volume. Cf. Mahābhārata, Āśvamedhika-parvan 793, &c.

[3] This is a hit at the S'rāddha, when (as we have explained at p. 66) oblations of cakes and libations of water are made to the spirits of deceased fathers, grandfathers, and progenitors.

[4] 'Let us eat and drink, for to-morrow we die' (1 Cor. xv. 32). Compare such Horatian precepts as Epod. xiii. 3, &c.

[5] Two curious Vedic words, *jarbharī* and *turpharī*, are given in the text as specimens of what I suppose modern scoffers might call 'Vedic slang. They occur in Ṛig-veda X. 106, 6, and

As a conclusion to our Appendix, we commend the foregoing curious commentary on the religious system of the Hindūs by an enemy within their own camp, to the special attention of the Christian Missionary in India. The satirical spirit it evinces is very different from that we have recommended, at the end of our 12th chapter, as likely to be most effective in contending with the Hydra Hindūism.

Nirukta XIII. 5. For their explanation, see Böhtlingk and Roth, and my Sanskrit-English Dictionary (published by Macmillan & Co. for the University of Oxford).

PRONUNCIATION OF LETTERS IN WORDS OF SANSKṚIT ORIGIN.

VOWELS.

a	as in	rur*a*l.	*ṛi*	as in	mer*ri*ly.
ā	,,	t*a*r, f*a*ther.	*ṛī*	,,	ma*ri*ne.
i	,,	f*i*ll.	*e*	,,	pr*e*y.
ī	,,	pol*i*ce.	*ai*	,,	*ai*sle.
u	,,	f*u*ll.	*o*	,,	g*o*.
ū	,,	r*u*de.	*au*	,,	H*au*s (German).

CONSONANTS.

k	as in	*k*ill, see*k*.
kh	,,	in*kh*orn.
g	,,	*g*un, do*g*.
gh	,,	lo*gh*ut.
n	before *k* or *g*, as in	si*n*k, si*n*g.
ĉ	as *ch* in	*ch*ur*ch* (*ĉ*ur*ĉ*).
ĉh	as *chh* in	chur*chh*ill.
j	as in	*j*et.
jh	as *dgeh* in	he*dgeh*og (he*jh*og).
n	before *c* and *j*, as in	i*n*ch, si*n*ge.
ṭ	as in	*t*rue.
ṭh	,,	an*th*ill.
ḍ	,,	*d*rum.
ḍh	,,	re*dh*aired.
ṇ	,,	*n*o*n*e.
t	,,	wa*t*er (in Ireland).
th	,,	nu*t-h*ook (but more dental).
d	,,	*d*ice (more like *th* in *th*is).
dh	,,	a*dh*ere (but more dental).
n	,,	*n*ot, i*n*
p	,,	*p*ut, si*p*.
ph	,,	u*ph*ill.
b	,,	*b*ear, ru*b*.
bh	,,	a*bh*or.
m	,,	*m*ap, ja*m*.
y	,,	*y*et.
r	,,	*r*ed, yea*r*.
l	,,	*l*ie.
v	,,	*v*ie (like *w* after consonants).
ś	,,	*s*ure, ses*s*ion.
sh	,,	*sh*un, hu*sh*.
s	,,	*s*ir, his*s*.
h	,,	*h*it.
ḥ	*i.e.* Visarga, or a distinctly audible aspirate.	

INDEX.

WYMAN AND SONS, PRINTERS, GREAT QUEEN-STREET, LONDON, W.C.

NON-CHRISTIAN RELIGIOUS SYSTEMS.

Fcap. 8vo., Cloth boards, price 2s. 6d. each, with Map.

BUDDHISM:

Being a Sketch of the Life and Teachings of Gautama, the Buddha. By T. W. RHYS DAVIDS, of the Middle Temple.

HINDUISM.

By MONIER WILLIAMS, M.A., D.C.L., &c.

ISLAM AND ITS FOUNDER.

By J. W. H. STOBART, B.A., Principal, La Martinière College, Lucknow.

THE HEATHEN WORLD AND ST. PAUL.

Fcap. 8vo., Cloth boards, price 2s. each, with Map.

ST. PAUL IN DAMASCUS AND ARABIA.

By the Rev. GEORGE RAWLINSON, M.A., Canon of Canterbury, Camden Professor of Ancient History, Oxford.

ST. PAUL IN GREECE.

By the Rev. G. S. DAVIES, M.A., Charterhouse, Godalming.

ST. PAUL AT ROME.

By the Very Rev. CHARLES MERIVALE, D.D., D.C.L., Dean of Ely.

ST. PAUL IN ASIA MINOR, AND AT THE SYRIAN ANTIOCH.

By the Rev. E. H. PLUMPTRE, D.D., Prebendary of St. Paul's, Vicar of Bickley, Kent, and Professor of New Testament Exegesis in King's College, London.

RECENT PUBLICATIONS.

	s.	d.
AFRICA UNVEILED. By the Rev. H. ROWLEY. With Map, and Eight full-page Illustrations on toned paper. Crown 8vo. .... *Cloth Boards*	5	0
BIBLE PLACES; OR, THE TOPOGRAPHY OF THE HOLY LAND: a Succinct Account of all the Places, Rivers, and Mountains of the Land of Israel mentioned in the Bible, so far as they have been identified. Together with their Modern Names and Historical References. By the Rev. Canon TRISTRAM. *A new and revised Edition, Crown 8vo., with Map, numerous Wood-cuts* .... *Cloth Boards*	4	0
CHINA: THE LAND AND THE PEOPLE OF. A short Account of the Geography, History, Religion, Social Life, Arts, Industries, and Government of China and its People. By J. THOMSON, Esq., F.R.G.S., Author of "Illustrations of China and its People," &c. With Map, and Twelve full-page Illustrations on toned paper. Crown 8vo. .... *Cloth Boards*	5	0
CHRISTIANS UNDER THE CRESCENT. By the Rev. E. L. CUTTS, B.A., Hon. D.D. University of the South, U.S., Author of "Turning Points of English and General Church History," &c. With numerous Illustrations. Post 8vo. *Cloth Boards*	5	0
INDIA: THE HISTORY OF, from the Earliest Times to the Present Day. By L. J. TROTTER, Author of "Studies in Biography." Post 8vo. With a Map and 23 Engravings .... *Cloth Boards*	10	6
ISRAEL: THE LAND OF. A Journal of Travels in Palestine, undertaken with Special Reference to its Physical Character. Third Edition, revised. By the Rev. Canon TRISTRAM. With numerous Illustrations .... *Cloth Boards*	10	6
JEWISH NATION: A HISTORY OF THE. From the Earliest Times to the Present Day. By E. H. PALMER, Esq., M.A., Fellow of St. John's College, and Lord Almoner's Professor of Arabic in the University of Cambridge, Author of "The Desert of the Exodus," &c. &c. Crown 8vo. With Map and numerous Illustrations .... *Cloth Boards*	5	0

	s.	d.
LESSER LIGHTS; or, Some of the Minor Characters of Scripture traced, with a View to Instruction and Example in Daily Life. By the Rev. F. BOURDILLON, M.A., Author of "Bedside Readings," &c. Post 8vo. ... *Cloth Boards*	2	6
NATURAL HISTORY OF THE BIBLE, THE: being a Review of the Physical Geography, Geology, and Meteorology of the Holy Land, with a description of every Animal and Plant mentioned in Holy Scripture. By the Rev. Canon TRISTRAM. Third Edition. Crown 8vo. With numerous Illustrations.......... *Cloth Boards*	7	6
NARRATIVE OF A MODERN PILGRIMAGE THROUGH PALESTINE ON HORSEBACK, AND WITH TENTS. By the Rev. ALFRED CHARLES SMITH, M.A., Christ Church, Oxford; Rector of Yatesbury, Wilts, Author of "The Attractions of the Nile," &c. &c. Crown 8vo. With numerous Illustrations and Four Coloured Plates .... *Cloth Boards*	5	0
SCENES IN THE EAST.—Containing Twelve Coloured Photographic Views of Places mentioned in the Bible. By the Rev. Canon TRISTRAM, Author of "The Land of Israel," &c. 4to. .... *Cloth Boards*	7	6
SCRIPTURE MANNERS AND CUSTOMS: being an Account of the Domestic Habits, Arts, &c., of Eastern Nations, mentioned in Holy Scripture. Sixteenth Edition. Fcap. 8vo. With numerous Wood-cuts .... *Cloth Boards*	4	0
SINAI AND JERUSALEM; or, Scenes from Bible Lands, consisting of Coloured Photographic Views of Places mentioned in the Bible, including a Panoramic View of Jerusalem. With Descriptive Letterpress by the Rev. F. W. HOLLAND, M.A., Honorary Secretary to the Palestine Exploration Fund .... *Cloth, Bevelled Boards, gilt edges*	7	6
ST. PAUL: THE CITIES VISITED BY. By the Rev. Professor STANLEY LEATHES, M.A., King's College, London. Fcap. 8vo. With Nine Wood-cuts .... *Limp cloth*	1	0
TURNING POINTS OF ENGLISH CHURCH HISTORY. By the Rev. EDWARD L. CUTTS, B.A., Author of "Some Chief Truths of Religion," "St. Cedd's Cross," &c. Crown 8vo. .... *Cloth Boards*	3	6
TURNING POINTS OF GENERAL CHURCH HISTORY. By the Rev. E. L. CUTTS, B.A., Author of "Pastoral Counsels," &c. Crown 8vo. .... *Cloth Boards*	5	0

www.ingramcontent.com/pod-product-compliance
Ingram Content Group UK Ltd.
Pitfield, Milton Keynes, MK11 3LW, UK
UKHW031312170225
4629UKWH00035B/445

9 783337 735371